JOEN WOLFROM

Adventures in
DESIGN

The Ultimate Visual Guide • 153 Spectacular Quilts • Activities & Exercises

C&T PUBLISHING

Text and Photography copyright © 2011 by Joen Wolfrom

Photography and Artwork copyright © 2011 by C&T Publishing, Inc.

Hand-drawn Illustrations copyright © 2011 by Kate Darnell

Publisher: Amy Marson

Creative Director: Gailen Runge

Acquisitions Editor: Susanne Woods

Editor: Liz Aneloski

Technical Editor: Sandy Peterson

Cover Designer: Kris Yenche

Book Designer: Kerry Graham

Production Coordinator: Jessica Jenkins

Production Editor: Alice Mace Nakanishi

Illustrator: Hand-drawn illustrations by Kate Darnell;
computer illustrations by Wendy Mathson

Quilt Photography by Christina Carty-Francis and Diane Pedersen
of C&T Publishing, Inc., unless otherwise noted

Nature and Illustrative Photography by Joen Wolfrom

Published by C&T Publishing, Inc., P.O. Box 1456, Lafayette, CA 94549

Library of Congress Cataloging-in-Publication Data

Wolfrom, Joen.

Adventures in design : the ultimate visual guide : 153 spectacular quilts : activities & exercises / Joen Wolfrom.

p. cm.

Includes bibliographical references and index.

ISBN 978-1-57120-860-6 (soft cover)

1. Patchwork--Patterns. 2. Patchwork--Design. I. Title.

TT835.W6437 2011

746.46--dc22

2010054232

Printed in China

10 9 8 7 6 5 4 3

DEDICATION

I dedicate this book to three generations of those most precious to me—Jack and Joseph Githens, Micah and Francess Wolfrom, Dane Wolfrom, Danielle and Mike Githens, Cheri and David Wolfrom, and Dan Wolfrom.

ACKNOWLEDGMENTS

I wish to thank my wonderful, patient, superb editor, Liz Aneloski. I am thankful for the hard work and expertise of the C&T Publishing staff. I am grateful to C&T Publishing for its interest in publishing *Adventures in Design*, which is my ninth book.

This book would not have been possible without the generous artists and quiltmakers who so willingly offered to share their artworks and quilts for this book. I am indebted to each of them, as they have enriched this book by allowing me to use their works as examples to illustrate nature's elements and principles of design. I could not have done it without them. I wish to thank those of you whose works grace the pages of this book:

Charlotte Warr Andersen • Alex Anderson • Frieda Anderson • Meredith Annett • Ludmila Aristova • Linda Beach • Sue Benner • Lies Bos-Varkevisser • Kathie Briggs • Janyce Broude • Karen Kay Buckley • Melinda Bula • Sally Collins • Sharyn Craig • Lenore Crawford • Linda Crouch-McCreadie • Judy Dales • Kate Darnell • Mickey Depre • Pat Durbin • Robbi Joy Eklow • Noriko Endo • Ann Fahl • Caryl Bryer Fallert • Anna Faustino • John Flynn • Wil Fritsma • Kay D. Haerland • Jane Hall • Robin Haller • Gloria Hansen • Denise Havlan • Marian Henstra • Bill Horn • Steen Hougs • Linda Kaiser • Ans Kastein • Annette Kennedy • Larisa Key • Cindy Kurey • Denise Labadie • Julie Lambert • Stacie Littlejohn • Allison Lockwood • Jane Loeffler • Gloria Loughman • Rosinah Mabasa • Irene MacWilliam • Gwen Magee • Inge Mardal • Beth Miller • Pamela Mostek • Scott Murkin • Paula Nadelstern • Sylvia Naylor • Sue Nickels • Judy and Brad Niemeyer • Barbara Ortiz • Mary Louise Parks • Helen Remick • Janett Rice • Amanda Richardson • Jane Sassaman • Norma Schlager • Jayne Willoughby Scott • Barbara Shapel • Judy Simmons • Judy Spiers • Janet Steadman • Margarete Steinhauer • Carol Taylor • Judy Tescher • Ricky Tims • Lorraine Torrence • Gwyned Trefethen • Dineke Ugen • Annette Valtl • Laura Wasilowski • Jean Wells Keenan • Rachel Wetzler • Darra Williamson • Colleen Wise

CONTENTS

Before Beginning

We live in a world surrounded by beautiful flawless examples of nature's design elements and principles. As you learn, study, and experiment with these fascinating design concepts, the doors to an exciting world will open before you. Enjoy each step of this amazing exploration, as you work from one chapter to the next.

In this book, Section One provides you with an in-depth look at each element of design. Section Two discusses the principles of design—those wonderful strategies and rules that help you create fantastic designs. Section Three features extra design information that is uniquely pertinent to quiltmakers and patchworkers. At the end of each chapter are activities and exercises that are relevant to the topics discussed. They are provided to give you opportunities to expand and explore the many components of design, as well as to become better acquainted with your personal design style and preferences.

Consider beginning your own artist's notebook or design journal. As you read this book and work through the activities and exercises, keep notes about ideas, images, or pictures that inspire you, as well as your own design ideas and comments. This notebook should be a great personal design reference.

Contributors Who Have Shared Their Works of Art

You may spend many hours absorbed in investigating the wondrous, imaginative designs between the covers of this book. Explore the works of the artists for ideas, inspiration, and reference. Many captions include invaluable insight into how specific design principles have been used.

Because you relate to art uniquely, it is important to have a broad spectrum of designs for you to refer to while exploring

your design ideas. For this reason, I have gathered as many different works of art as possible to illustrate nature's design concepts. I am indebted to the artists and craftspersons who have agreed to share their talents and beautiful designs. Their generosity has been overwhelming.

Explore the talents and additional works of these artists by visiting their websites to view their other works and products. Contributors are from the United States, Canada, Australia, England, Northern Ireland, the Netherlands, Germany, South Africa, France, and Japan. Some contributors show the influence of their native land or other nations with which they have had close ties, such as the Republic of Ireland, Denmark, and Russia. Within the vast, geographically diverse United States and Canada, artists reside in many states and several provinces. Therefore, you will see a diverse selection of design styles and artistic flavors.

A Note about the Artwork and Illustrations

This book includes artwork in two galleries and within the pages of all but the first chapter. Artwork has been placed within a chapter because it is relevant to the discussion in that particular chapter. However, almost all of the artwork is relevant to more than one topic. Therefore, you will find within each chapter many references to artwork on a specific page in a gallery or in another chapter. If you do not like thumbing through the pages to view the referenced examples, do not feel obliged to do so. Give yourself permission not to take part in viewing these references if it bothers you. However, if you want to get the most out of the concepts presented, I highly recommend that you view the referenced artwork in the galleries and chapters as you read.

It is with great excitement that I share this book with you. I hope you enjoy its offerings. Happy designing!

Joen

THE CALM AFTER THE STORM by Inge Mardal and Steen Hougs, Chantilly, France, 49″ × 49″, 2009

This stunning piece is artfully balanced in its setting. In this realistic imagery, the balance has been beautifully achieved by a triangular structure that uses the three raincoat images for its endpoints. This structure allows our eyes to move from one figure to the other in the boat, then down to the reflected figure in the water, and back up to the first figure in the boat in a clockwise directional flow. The intricate quilting by Inge creates further interest and dimension. The broken-up reflection connotes movement through gentle wave action.

Photo by the artist

I'VE BEEN TO MECCA by Robin M. Haller, Carbondale, Illinois, 102″ × 82″, 2001

Robin used the historic North Wind block design to create *I've Been to Mecca*. This quilt uses value as its featured element, moving from rich dark hues to softly colored light hues.

Photo by the artist

FIVE APPLES by Pamela Mostek, Cheney, Washington, 47″ × 29″, 2008

Pamela, inspired by the Renaissance painters and their use of chiaroscuro (using the strong value contrast of light and dark—*clear/obscure*—as the dominant means to define three-dimensional shapes), created *Five Apples*, which illustrates the beautiful effect of light and shadow in this pictorial representation. The use of an uneven number of apples allows our eyes to find a focus point, which provides visual comfort. Pamela's fabric selection allows for exceptional textural effects. Luster is created through the use of gradual value change. *Five Apples* won both a judge's award and a juror's award at the 2008 Association of Pacific Northwest Quilters show in Seattle, Washington.

STAR OF WONDER designed and quilted by Linda Crouch-McCreadie, Jonesborough, Tennessee; pieced by Renny Jaeger; 70″ × 90″, 2010

By putting the Star Echoes block in a diagonal setting, Linda gave the star a beautiful facelift (page 123). The golden four-pointed star appears to be behind the other star layers because it is lighter and grayer (more toned) than the other stars. To further enhance the quilt, Linda created a border that allows the central design to be featured.

HOUSE THROUGH ARCH by Lenore Crawford, Midland, Michigan, 38″ × 44″, 2006

This impressionistic scene brilliantly uses value to great effect to create the marvelous illusion of the house through the arch. The repeating curves in the design provide harmony, rhythm, and unity. The dark left side is counterbalanced by the beautiful coppery strong archway and the creamy foreground wall on the right. Notice how Lenore helps balance the darkness of the door with a dark brown vertical shadow on the right side. The flowers flow beautifully through the design. This scene is filled with wonderful textures created by Lenore's selection of fabrics. The design is made from 2″ pieced squares.

TROPICAL RADIANCE by Rachel Wetzler, St. Charles, Illinois, 64″ × 64″, 2008

This quilt's analogous color plan provides natural harmony. Repetition of the four-pointed stars and their echoing throughout the piece brings unity to the design. The inner diagonal border offers interesting contrast. Notice how this design radiates from the center, creating beautiful balance. This quilt was inspired by the traditional quilt design The Palm, but was altered for paper piecing.

WATER CURTAIN WITH ORCHIDS
by Amanda Richardson, Cornwall, England,
78″ × 60″, 2006

Water Curtain with Orchids is beautifully realistic in its garden interpretation. Amanda was able to create wonderful textures by using a wide variety of fabrics. Notice how your eyes move in a circular clockwise manner through this design. Also, notice how the large stone at the bottom right is counterbalanced by the brightly colored orchids, the water curtain, and the white orchids. This close view of a magnificent garden scene illustrates many design principles with regard to both unity and asymmetrical balance. After becoming more familiar with these principles, revisit this artwork to observe further how Amanda effectively brought balance and unity to this lovely garden scene.

AUTUMN WALK by Noriko Endo, Tokyo, Japan, 90″ × 48″, 2002

Noriko's textured landscapes are breathtaking works of art, and *Autumn Walk* is particularly inviting with its analogous fall colors so effectively drawing us into the scene. The oblique lines of the trees carry our eyes down the pathway. The stunningly textured leaves are ablaze with colors that subtly reiterate the coloring of the angled tree-lined pathway. The dark brown tree trunks offer richly colored contrast. This is definitely an autumn walk that you don't want to miss! (If you are mesmerized by Noriko's use of texture, refer to her book *Confetti Naturescapes*.) Notice that the brilliance of the textured leaves is most intense in the foreground. As the trees move down the pathway, the colors become more subdued. Also notice that the autumnal hues on the ground are toned rather than brilliant. Capturing the subtle nuances in nature is one of Noriko's wonderful talents.

Setting the Visual Stage

EIGHT INGREDIENTS FOR GREAT DESIGNS

CHAPTER ONE

The POWER of DESIGN Speaking the Language

Clearly there is no one right way to create a design that fascinates or satisfies everyone. There is, however, an established manner of working that increases the beauty and success of any design. You can achieve great design success by observing nature at work and using her as your visual guide. *Adventures in Design* is a presentation of nature's design basics to help you build a design foundation from which you can develop your personal style.

It is a dramatic turning point in our artistic pathway when we come to the realization that a design that beckons us to pause and admire its beauty was not haphazardly created. Instead, its magical draw is a blend of imagination and nature's design basics. Knowing these wonderful design secrets gives you the freedom to create designs with amazing success.

Being Your Artistic Self

Designing your own art, no matter the medium, is an expression of *your* creative soul. Your instinctive design style emerges from a combination of your innate personality, lifetime experiences, surroundings, reflections, and sensibilities.

No one piece of art or single style is right for everyone. It does not matter, then, if your taste differs from that of others. Most assuredly, it is of little consequence or importance if you find yourself alone in your likes. Recognizing what styles of art you want to create and surround yourself with is one of the most important gifts you can give yourself.

Because you use design to express yourself and tell your visual story, it is important to know what captures your spirit, what makes you excited, and what you think is beautiful or stunning.

You should recognize whether you prefer busyness and complexity or clean lines and simplicity, gentle or dramatic hues, sharp or soft edges, or angular or curved shapes, to name a few preferences. To recognize your preferences and innate style, it is important for you to actively view all kinds of art; this will broaden your scope and give your imagination a banquet of ideas to feast on.

CREATING BEAUTIFUL ART

All beautiful art is made up of design elements. By name, these elements are *line, direction, shape (form), color, value, texture, proportion,* and *scale.* Consider these elements as your personal design team. Each of these team members will play a part in your design. When you begin your design, you will decide which element plays the leading role, which one has a secondary position, and in what way the other elements may support or enhance the design. As the designer, your role is to manage these individual team players so that they blend into a beautiful visual statement.

In design, if the elements are allowed to do whatever they want, there is visual noise—better known as visual chaos. One element cannot be allowed to become so distracting that it overwhelms the other members of the design team. Two elements competing against each other for attention are distracting. As the designer, it is your task to determine how the team members play together; which one to feature; which one, if any, is a secondary player; and which ones simply support and enhance.

As with any team, there are rules and strategies to help you succeed. In art, these rules and strategies are commonly referred to as the *principles of design. Unity* is a key principle in a successful design, but it needs help from other principles to exist. These ancillary principles that help create unity and visually strengthen a design are *repetition, rhythm, harmony, variation, contrast, bridging, proximity, movement,* and *dominance.* Some are needed in every design while others are included when invited. *Balance* and *focus,* two additional principles, have tremendous power and responsibility in the visual success of a design. Although they both can vary in their nature, their existence in a successful design is essential.

Understanding the elements and principles gives you design power. Knowing how to use them in interesting ways allows you to achieve strong visual success.

With these thoughts in mind, it's now time to begin this adventure in design.

CHAPTER TWO

SETTING THE STAGE
Through Line *and* Direction

How do you begin a design? What decisions come first? It's much like the question of the chicken and the egg. Although your inspiration may come from any one of the elements of design (page 13), the essence of your design most likely begins with *line*—the element that provides the simplest, most effective way to make your design possible.

Line can be a star in its own right without any help from other elements. Pen-and-ink drawings and cartoons are excellent examples of line creating visual suggestions. It's amazing how different lines can create different imagery, as shown to the right.

Fat, thin, short, long, curved, straight, jagged—there are so many choices with which to interpret a design. Line is like a chameleon in the way it can change. Its interpretive powers are limitless. Line is present in every design, yet it changes its character and style from one design to another. It can evoke a sense of excitement, curiosity, apprehension, awe, power, calmness, perfection, or peace. Movement or stillness, strength or weakness, happiness or anger—all can be shown through line.

A delicate line; a short pointillist stroke; a strong, wide brushstroke—all create different visual effects.

Line can be used to define edges, make contours, and create a wide array of shapes.

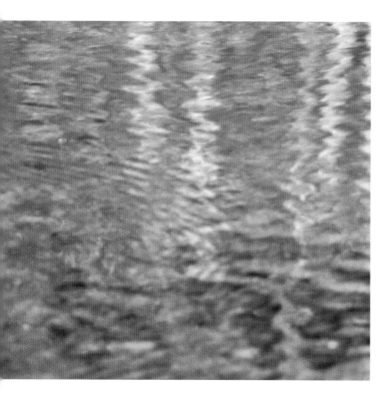

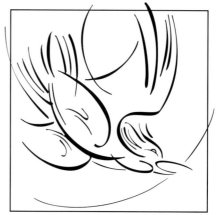

Line can be used to convey the idea of direction and movement.

Finding Star Power in Line

Besides its interpretive powers, line's most important roles are to define shapes and promote direction. Line can be well defined, blurred, implied, partially apparent, or primarily hidden. Usually line partners with other elements to create a design. Color often acts as the primary element to move line in a particular direction.

Line can innovatively partner with shapes to show direction and movement.

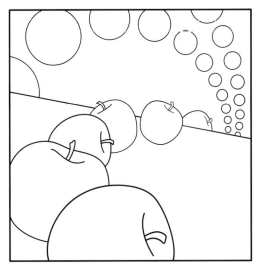

Line defines shapes. It can then use these shapes to create direction and movement.

Line can use color to define shapes and create direction or movement.

It's possible for value to play the leading role as the conduit for line to create shapes, direction, and movement.

Also, line can be used to create a variety of textures, creating interest along with direction and movement.

Line can create a wide array of textures. Texture can show detail, direction, and movement.

Line can use value to play a major role in defining shapes and creating direction or promoting movement.

Although direction is an element, it is the action of line that creates direction. The fascinating visual possibilities are endless when line forms a partnership with other closely related elements.

When you begin thinking about your design, consider which elements (page 13) will work best to create your vision. Your choice will depend on the visual story you want to tell and how you want to tell that story. The following are important factors to consider when selecting the line style most appropriate for your design.

Line's Multiple Personalities

Line and direction set the pace for carrying the eye from one area of a design to another. Because the direction of line can elicit different emotions and effects, what you do with line is an important consideration. Line can be categorized into five broad groups. These major *line styles* determine the line direction within a design: vertical, horizontal, diagonal (or oblique), closed curve (circular), and open curve. Understanding the differences between these line styles will be extremely helpful in your design process. It will allow you to select the line style that provides the best vehicle to convey the visual story you wish to tell.

LINE WITH VERTICAL DIRECTION

Vertical line is the king of linear strength. It's bold and powerful. If you want your design to be visually powerful, create a design featuring vertical line. New York City, San Francisco, and other large, vibrant cities reflect power and strength with their skyscrapers standing high in the sky. Cities with low horizontal profiles do not convey the same visual power. Cottonwood and aspen trees cannot compete with giant sequoias for power and awe. Towering trees, skyscrapers, cathedral spires, mountain peaks, and other tall vertical structures illustrate the visual power and strength subconsciously given to vertical line.

Tall objects exude a sense of power over shorter objects, as seen here with Seattle's Space Needle.

Pat Durbin's *Winter Walk* is a great example of power in vertical line. The vertical length in *Acid Rain* (page 80) is important to its visual story too.

Vertical line can also evoke a feeling of elegant and sophisticated power. *Dressed for the Party* beautifully illustrates the elegance and sophistication of vertical line. Other designs using vertical line to great advantage are *Moonlight Sonata* and *Weeping Willow over Water* (pages 49 and 83).

DRESSED FOR THE PARTY by Ans Kastein, Didam, the Netherlands, 33½″ × 59″, 2007

In this surreal artwork inspired by Klimt, Ans has created a design with strong vertical line. The strength of the vertical line is accentuated by its vertical format. The repetition of color and shape creates pattern, harmony, and unity.

Photo by Photostudio Marks, Didam, the Netherlands

WINTER WALK by Pat Durbin, Eureka, California, 16″ × 42″, 2007

The power of this giant tree is realized by its strong vertical line. Placing this design in a narrow vertical rectangle accentuates its strength. The texture of the tree trunk and the exquisite needle art used for the greenery are superb.

Photo by Gary A. Durbin

If you are drawn to vertical line but prefer to use it to convey a soft visual statement, lessen its natural strength by using muted colors and subtle value contrasts.

By muting colors and lessening value contrast, the power of vertical line and vertically oblique lines can be softened.

This quieter effect of vertical line can be seen in Lenore Crawford's *A City Walk in Spring* (page 84).

Most vertical designs are best placed in a vertical format, as it accentuates the vertical direction and provides for better use of the design surface.

LINE WITH HORIZONTAL DIRECTION

Horizontal line provides a natural overall calming effect, as seen here on a Northumberland, England, shoreline.

If your design's line moves in a horizontal direction, it has a natural inclination to be calming and restful. Horizontal line lends itself beautifully to landscapes with a horizontal flow of meadows, hills, mountain ranges, plains, farmlands, gardens, deserts, and water. *Sunrise over Tuscany* (page 18) is a superb example of calmness accentuated by horizontal line reiterated in sky, distant hills, close green hills in fog, and foreground.

In Beth Miller's *The Girls of Tyrone Farm* (page 88), the design is broken into three informal horizontal divisions: sky, grassy hill, and fence. The fourth horizontal line is provided by the featured girls with their bodies reiterating the suggestion of horizontal line. The horizontal line remains visually dominant while the background trees provide directional contrast. *Springtime in the Valley* (page 44) provides the quiet calm of horizontal line with the mountain range, the bulb fields, and the sky at sunrise.

You can override horizontal line's natural restful bias by incorporating strong colors and value contrast, large or flamboyant shapes, or other eye-catching effects. For instance, *Marsh #18: Sunny Day* (page 18) illustrates how easily strong coloring can create a spirited, joyous effect, overriding the natural inclination toward restfulness. *Poulnabrone Dolmen* (page 91), a hauntingly beautiful design, is a horizontal design evoking dramatic visual strength because of its large shapes, strong value contrast, and somber coloring.

Horizontal designs are most comfortable in a horizontal format or setting. Also, vertical objects presented horizontally across the design surface usually call for a horizontal setting. For example, the vertical flowers in *Dresden Flower Garden* (page 89) are placed in an informal horizontal line that moves the viewer's eyes horizontally across the design's surface.

MARSH #18: SUNNY DAY by Sue Benner, Dallas, Texas, 62″ × 14″, 2006

In this sunny impressionistic design, the horizontal lines create unity throughout. The vertical lines provide both variation and contrast. Sue chose brilliant colors to override the natural horizontal-line calmness, giving her design a joyous spirit. She created this scene in a 4.5:1 ratio (pages 77–81). This allowed her to expand the breadth of her horizontal design while limiting the vertical view to what she deemed most essential.

Photo by Eric J. Neilsen, Eric Neilsen Photography, Dallas, Texas

SUNRISE OVER TUSCANY by Lenore Crawford, Midland, Michigan, 36″ × 22″, 2007

The morning calmness is accentuated by the horizontal layers in this design: sky, distant hills, close hills, rolling fog, and farmland. The house, with its warm hues, provides contrast and added interest. The quilting lines add richness to this beautiful scene. *Sunrise over Tuscany* uses a modified triadic color plan.

Photo by the artist

DIAGONAL AND OBLIQUE LINES

Diagonal, oblique, or slanted line can create visual excitement, intrigue, and movement. A line's angle can vary, but the result is the same—the line moves the eye through the design's surface.

A diagonal or oblique line creates natural movement and direction.

Diagonal line can be both dramatic and subtle. Its magical possibilities are endless. One of its premier visual characteristics is its ability to promote the appearance of movement. In *Yellow Poppies,* it appears as if the wind is blowing with the flowers bending in a diagonal line. Diagonal line often uses the elements of color and value to create its movement. Both color and value are used to create the movement in *Malalani,* whereas only color provides the diagonal line in *Pizzazz* (page 43). The former design uses both subtle and bold contrasts. In *Eye-Catching Eyespot* (page 80), the broken line gently leads our eyes diagonally away from and toward the butterfly. The two converging oblique lines of trees in Noriko Endo's *Autumn Walk* (page 11) invite our eyes to take a walk through the trees.

MALALANI by Jane Loeffler, Makawao, Hawaii; quilted by Cathy Franks; 103″ × 113″, 1998

Combining subtle curves with diagonal line creates beautiful movement in *Malalani.* Color change, along with value contrast, helps move our eyes along the diagonal pathways.

Photo by Randy Hufford, Kula, Hawaii

YELLOW POPPIES by Lenore Crawford, Midland, Michigan, 25″ × 18″, 2009

Because these luscious poppies are placed in an oblique position, we assume there is wind or movement of some sort. Lenore uses subtle value steps to create a sense of luster and shadows in her poppies. She has added beautiful texture through her thread-work. (Pattern is available.)

Photo by the artist

Diagonal line can be dramatic and visually exciting when it changes direction within the design, as in *Northern Lights.* The more frequently the diagonal line changes direction, the stronger the attraction and the more dramatic the design is. A stunning example of diagonal line changing direction is Caryl Bryer Fallert's *High Tech Tucks #35* (page 106). Notice how effectively your eyes move across the design. If you love strong movement, consider changing direction in your diagonal design to add extra movement and visual drama.

NORTHERN LIGHTS by Joen Wolfrom, Fox Island, Washington; quilted by Veronica Nurmi, Mt. Shasta, California; 70″ × 70″, 2005

Northern Lights uses diagonal lines from two directions, which intensifies the sense of movement. This design is further enhanced by the use of a four-step value change in each block, resulting in luster and deep shading. (Pattern is available.)

Photo by Ken Wagner, Seattle, Washington

If your diagonal line moves horizontally across the surface, place it in a horizontal format; if it moves vertically, place it in a vertical setting. Some diagonal designs will look best in a square format. Choose the format that best suits your design.

CLOSED CURVES

A circle is made from a closed-curve line. Circular designs are controlled and well balanced. Circles provide a sense of completion, perfection, and beauty, which brings visual satisfaction.

Closed curves create a sense of balance, perfection, completeness, and beauty, as seen in many flowers.

Cheddar Cheese (page 21), a contemporary rendition of a kaleidoscope, is an excellent example of a beautifully controlled circular design.

Circular designs can be simple or intricate, delicate or strong. The design possibilities are endless when you consider the divisional choices within the 360° of a circle. Add to that all the intricacies that can be developed through the addition of concentric circles. Other magnificent examples of circular designs are *Primrose, Amazon Star, Sedona, Rosa Celeste, Dream of Infinity, Pineapple Surprise Again,* and *Bright Hopes* (pages 37, 58, 59, 70, 103, 108, and 138). They are all so different, yet their circular similarities are very apparent. Circular designs are most comfortable in a square setting.

If you elongate the closed circle so it becomes an oval, additional innovative opportunities for exciting, dynamic designs evolve. A stunning example of an elliptical design is Margarete Steinhauer's *Tsunami* (page 23).

CHEDDAR CHEESE by Paula Nadelstern, Bronx, New York, 20″ × 20″, 2008

A master at creating kaleidoscopic designs, Paula has produced a stunning circular design that provides a sense of both perfection and completion. The interior points move our eyes from the center to the outermost points. Our eyes are particularly captivated when intricate detailing exists, as shown in this design.

OPEN CURVES

Open curving lines promote flowing movement throughout the design.

Beautiful open curves create a sense of fluidity with our eyes moving along the flowing curves, as they do with these sand dunes in Death Valley.

Open curves are the most free-spirited personalities of all the line styles. The design options vary greatly. Only the imagination limits the possibilities. Caryl Bryer Fallert's *Midnight Fantasy #6* is a beautiful design that shows the fluidity that open curves provide. *Feathers in the Wind* (page 85), another fantastic artwork by Caryl, shows the versatility of both Caryl's creativity and open-curve designs.

MIDNIGHT FANTASY #6 by Caryl Bryer Fallert, Paducah, Kentucky, 48" × 59", 2003

Caryl's beautiful curving lines flow throughout the design, causing our eyes to move along with them. This design uses a primary triadic color plan. The textures created by the quilting stitch are stunning in this artwork.

Photo by the artist

Another beautiful example of open-curve designs can be seen in *Nemo's Ecstasy.* Other diverse examples include *Minor Miracle, Daydreams, Floral Forms I,* and *African Dreams* (pages 31, 67, 87, and 101).

NEMO'S ECSTASY by Lorraine Torrence, Seattle, Washington, 42" × 45", 1997

Nemo's Ecstasy uses open, free-flowing curved lines to create its design. This allows our eyes to move through the design. Lorraine has added geometric shapes for contrast. This quilt was designed for Lorraine's book *Design Essentials: The Quilter's Guide.*

TWO'S COMPANY; THREE'S A CROWD

If you include two or more different line styles in one design, one should be visually dominant. Thus, if you are using both vertical and diagonal lines in your design, one should play the dominant role and the other should be assigned either a secondary role or a minor position. The large circle in Dineke Ugen's *Dream of Infinity* (page 103) is dominant over the vertical rectangle. The vertical design in *Dandelions and Rust* (page 62) is visually stronger than the horizontal lines. The open curves are dominant over the vertical lines in *House through Arch* (page 9). The strong elliptical lines are dominant over the horizontal lines in *Tsunami* (page 23).

Use the secondary line to increase interest and add contrast. Never allow it enough strength to be in competition with your intended dominant line.

TSUNAMI by Margarete Steinhauer, Estes Park, Colorado, 43″ × 41″, 2006

This mirror-image design is a beautiful example of bilateral symmetry, using elliptical lines, gorgeous textures, color, and value to create electrifying movement. Notice the subtle ways Margarete used contrast and variation. *Tsunami* won first place honors in the Small Abstract Art category at the 2006 International Quilt Association show in Houston.

Selecting Your Design's Best Format

The decision to place your design in a vertical, horizontal, or square format depends on your design's direction of line. View the artwork in this chapter to see how the format accentuates each design's line and directional movement. Select your design's format to reflect its *overall linear direction,* so your design will maximize its visual potential. A design with strong vertical line shows its strength most effectively set in a vertical rectangle, as you can see in the vertically lined designs in this book. Horizontal movement or direction calls for a horizontal format. Repeating the design's dominant linear direction in its format accentuates the line and strengthens the design's visual beauty.

A square format doesn't provide direction on its own. It needs you to fill in the space; it's in limbo until you take action. Circular designs are best presented in a square format. They look awkward in a rectangular configuration.

It's challenging to use a square format with an asymmetrical design because it's a difficult feat to create visual balance. You will find most asymmetrical designs are in a horizontal or vertical rectangle, such as *House through Arch* and *Summer Rain* (pages 9 and 86). However, there are exceptions. Linda Beach placed her tree off-center in a square to create visual balance in *Oak Veiling* (page 113).

The mountains, hills, and water create a beautifully restful scene in *Monterey at Dusk.* Their horizontal lines are repeated with the numerous sailboats lying horizontally on the water. This design's dominant line is horizontal. Additional interest is provided through the contrasting secondary vertical lines of the sailboat masts.

Photo by the artist

MONTEREY AT DUSK by Melinda Bula, El Dorado Hills, California, 51″ × 60″, 2007

This impressionistic scene offers numerous types of horizontal lines that create a beautiful, restful scene. The repetition of horizontal line provides unity throughout. Contrast is created with the vertical masts. The quilting stitch adds texture. *Monterey at Dusk* won Best of Show at the 2008 Road to California exhibit in Ontario, California.

In *Dun Aengus Stone Fort*, Denise Labadie selected a vertical format. With this vertical format, the fort's vertical doorway is emphasized more than its horizontal stonework. The more extended the vertical rectangle, the more pronounced the doorway becomes. If Denise had wanted to feature the stonework, she would have had to place this design in a horizontal setting. This format change would cause our eyes to focus on the stonework, so that we would hardly notice the doorway. If Denise had placed this design in a square format, our eyes would flit from stonework to doorway, not knowing where to focus. This ambiguity would be visually unsettling. Happily, Denise chose her design focus and then selected the best format to reflect her decision.

DUN AENGUS STONE FORT by Denise Labadie, Longmont, Colorado, 63" × 71", 2006

Notice that this stone fort scene is placed in a vertical format. This compels our eyes to look through the vertical doorway to the vista beyond (see above for more information). The selection of fabrics used is amazing. This beautiful artwork received the People's Choice Award and Award for Craftsmanship at Quilt National 2007.

Photo by Esmond Snell

Interestingly, a scene of vertical trees in a horizontal format is interpreted by our eyes as a horizontal grouping of trees, as in *Autumn Orchard* (page 69). In contrast, a scene with a close-up view of tree trunks placed in a horizontal format will lead the eye through the trees' vertical lines to a place beyond. You can see this in *Setting Sun, Rising Moon* (page 102). Here our eyes go beyond the trees to the moon and the mountains. Linda Beach used the trees as an evocative enhancement rather than a focus. However, if the scene had been placed in a vertical format, our eyes would focus on the trees rather than the mountains and moon.

In *Sylvan Ambience* (page 26), notice how your eyes naturally go past the large foreground trees to the wooded area behind. This shift of focus can be used with any strong vertical lines placed in a horizontal format. As the artist, you have the power to choose what you want viewers to see in your design. This choice should help to determine your format.

If you are working with specific parameters such as a vertical wall, a king-size bed top, or a computer monitor, your first step will be to determine your format. Then create a design that works within your parameters. When working in this manner, your format will define the line options for your design.

With a bit of planning, line can help you create wonderful designs. Give yourself time to play with line, so that you can recognize your line preferences. Your designs will be the better for it.

SYLVAN AMBIENCE by Noriko Endo, Tokyo, Japan, 78″ × 54″, 2006

This horizontal presentation allows our eyes the luxury of finding interest behind the foreground trees in the woodland beyond with all its intriguing textures and subtle colorations. Noriko is a master at working with texture in beautiful woodland scenes. *Sylvan Ambience* is no exception, as this art-work is not only stunning, but Noriko's creation of asymmetrical balance through the placement of trees, color use, value, and texture is masterfully accomplished. After reading the asymmetrical balance information in Chapter 9 (page 108), do revisit *Sylvan Ambience* to observe how this scene's balance was created. Materials include cotton, luminescent fibers, tulle, and acrylic paint.

ACTIVITIES, EXERCISES, AND SUGGESTIONS

Line is one of the most important tools in designing. Begin focusing on line in all types of art. Select the activities listed below that most interest you or that you think will be most valuable.

1. Within a month's time, visit two to four galleries and museums. Or, look at the artwork (other than your own) in your home. Determine how line is used in the designs you particularly like. How does line partner with other elements to create the design? For each design that captures your imagination, jot down the important details of what you like: the type of line used, the direction, the way other elements are used, the format. Note if there was line/format compatibility (pages 24 and 25).

Also, notice the designs that are the most distracting to you. Jot down what displeases you about these designs. How do these designs work with line, direction, and other elements? Is there line/format compatibility? Determine what bothers you about each design. Analyze the differences between the designs you liked and those you didn't.

2. Place a selection of your own designs in front of you (originals or photos of your originals). Divide these images into three groups: your *favorites* group, your *not-so-happy-with* group, and your *just okay* group.

Analyze the designs in your *favorites* group. What do you observe? Write down what you notice about your use of line, direction, format, and so on. What are the similarities and differences between these designs? Next, take a look at the *not-so-happy-with* group. Write down what you notice about each of these designs. What do you believe their design problems are? Are they consistent from one design to another or are there different problems with each design? After analyzing these two groups and writing down your findings, ask yourself: What are you doing well in your designing? What changes do you need to make? In what areas do you need to acquire more expertise? Write down your findings. Next, go to the *just okay* group. For each, decide what you could have done to make it join your *favorites* group.

3. Visit your garden, your neighborhood surroundings, or a park with a digital camera in hand. Shoot as many images as you can to illustrate vertical line, horizontal line, diagonal line, closed curves, and open curves. Be imaginative with your picture taking. You may shoot your best images when looking at glimpses or details.

Download the images onto your computer. Select one image and make three copies of the original in your photo-editing software program. Crop each copy of the photo to make the best image possible in a horizontal format, a vertical format, and a square format. The square format will be the most challenging for almost all images. Be innovative in your cropping. It may be that by the time you are finished cropping, the image looks quite different from the original or is almost unrecognizable. Work on as many images as you can. You will learn so much about line, direction, movement, and format by playing with these images. After you are finished, select your favorite five redesigned images. Print your favorites along with the original photos. Display them together on paper. Keep for future reference. Repeat this exercise often.

4. Go to your computer and explore the amazing array of fonts available in your word-processing program (such as Microsoft Word). Select a minimum of six font types that have different, interesting design lines. From this group, select one font. Type a single letter in upper or lower case (your choice) in the largest font size available. Enlarge the letter to approximately 6"–8" high and make three copies. With a pencil, ruler, flexible curve, compass, protractor, and other drawing tools, begin playing with the letter, creating a design that evolves from the letter's lines. When you've finished the design, the original letter may have disappeared. Decide if your design is best served in a vertical, horizontal, or square format. Then draw the design's perimeter lines. Make two completely different new designs using the same letter, but create designs to fit the two remaining formats. When you have finished, mount your favorite design(s) on paper. You can vary this exercise by using two or more letters, numbers, or words.

CHAPTER THREE

SHAPE
Creating Design *and* Style

While line supplies your design with its foundation, *shapes* provide the means to create your design. Shapes are the workhorses in a design. Although the world is made up of an unbelievable array of shapes, most shapes can be grouped into four major categories:

- representational
- geometric
- organic
- nonobjective

In all likelihood, you will have an affinity for one of these categories. In this chapter the categories of shapes and their partnering *design styles* will be discussed.

Appealing to Your Sense of Shape

Representational shapes are those that represent something—either natural or man-made. *Mountain Chapel* is an example of a design using representational shapes. Other examples include *Georgette Tulips, Reflections, Playing Soccer,* and *Footloose* (pages 32, 33, and 35). *It's About Time* and *The Wedding Quilt* (both on page 34) combine representational shapes with geometric shapes.

MOUNTAIN CHAPEL by Annette Kennedy, Longmont, Colorado, 43″ × 53″, 2008

This glorious scene featuring a mountain chapel is an example of realism—representational art that appears as if it is a photograph or is nearly picture-perfect. Annette's attention to detail throughout is extraordinary. Her intricate stonework and windows are wonderful in their lifelike replication.

Photo by the artist

Geometric shapes are fascinating in their ability to work within all design styles. Interesting designs can be made from one or more geometric shapes. The basic repertoire of geometric shapes includes squares, rectangles, triangles, and circles. When you add trapezoids, diamonds, kites, rhombuses, hexagons, octagons, heptagons, and ellipses to the mix, you'll find yourself awash in a lifetime supply of geometric design possibilities. *Postage Stamp Baskets* and *Woodlands* are made from geometric shapes. *A Matter of Perspective* (page 30) is also made from geometric shapes. *It's About Time* and *The Wedding Quilt* (both on page 34) combine geometric shapes with representational shapes to create their designs.

POSTAGE STAMP BASKETS by Alex Anderson, Livermore, California, 57″ × 57″, 1994

In *Postage Stamp Baskets* Alex used geometric shapes to create representational shapes (the baskets). These baskets provide unity throughout the design. The interesting value change provides variation and contrast.

WOODLANDS by Darra Williamson, Walnut Creek, California, 51″ × 51″, 1992

Woodlands uses geometric shapes to create an abstract design of a wooded autumnal scene in the Blue Ridge Mountains of North Carolina. A split-complementary color plan was used to convey the woodland's soft autumn colors under the blue sky.

A MATTER OF PERSPECTIVE by Rachel Wetzler, St. Charles, Illinois, 46" × 46", 2000

In this design, Rachel uses geometric shapes in a very creative manner. The repetition of the elegant star creates a visual dance across the surface of the design. The interplay between large and small stars provides dynamic movement. Rhythm, harmony, and unity are present as well as beautiful symmetrical balance. The complementary golden yellow and blue-violet show what beautiful companions they are in a design.

Photo by the artist

Organic shapes are made from open-curve lines. Although they are similar to circles and ovals, they are free-flowing, so they are not bound by any geometric requirements. *Minor Miracle* (next page) is made from organic shapes. Others made from organic shapes include *Midnight Fantasy #6, Nemo's Ecstasy, Georgette Tulips, Blue Ginkgoes,* and *Feathers in the Wind* (pages 22, 32, 48, and 85).

CELLULAR STRUCTURE VIII (OVAL SHIFT) by Sue Benner, Dallas, Texas, 52″ × 70″, 2007

Cellular Structure VIII (Oval Shift) is created for pure visual enjoyment. Neither the shapes nor the design represents any objects or ideas for us to interpret. This is a beautiful example of nonobjective shapes being used to create an artwork in the nonobjective design style. The triadic color plan, textural effects, and value contrasts play an important role in this artwork's beauty.

Photo by Eric J. Neilsen, Eric Neilsen Photography, Dallas, Texas

SELECTING YOUR DESIGN'S SHAPES

You may choose to include only one category of shapes in your design or you may choose to combine categories. When you begin visualizing a design, think about which category of shapes will work best for you. If you need to integrate two or more categories, do so. Make certain, however, that one category of shapes is visually dominant.

MINOR MIRACLE by Jane A. Sassaman, Harvard, Illinois, 30″ × 48″, 1999

Jane used organic shapes to create this fanciful design in the broad representational design style. This intriguing design is truly a visual story with many tales. Jane has given us wonderful repetitious shapes to create unity throughout. The red roots form a rhythmic pattern of their own. The bulb gives great contrast with its straight lines and sharp points. The large periwinkle dots bring more variation. Jane has used a 5:8 ratio for this design (pages 77–81).

Photo by Gregory Gantner, Harvard, Illinois

Nonobjective shapes are oddly formed shapes that do not fit neatly into any other category. They can be blobs, squiggly forms, or weird, unrecognizable shapes. Any shape you can imagine that does not fit into any other group is a nonobjective shape. A nonobjective shape, *as a stand-alone shape,* has no meaning—it does not represent anything. These shapes are used most often in noninterpretive, nonobjective designs such as *Cellular Structure VIII (Oval Shift).* Additionally, nonobjective shapes can be used within a design to represent an object. You can see all sorts of nonobjective shapes in the representational design *5 of Clubs* (page 89). In *Summer Rain* (page 86), nonobjective shapes join together with color to create an illusion of a summer garden.

Your Intuitive Design Style

Knowing how you are going to work with shapes is a major decision in your design process. Not only do you have preferences for certain shapes, but you have preferences for the way a design is created—its design style. Assessing your design style preferences is an important part of design. Below are some basic guidelines to follow in determining what type of art speaks to your creative spirit.

Admittedly, there is a confusing array of names given to design styles that are really quite similar in makeup. Some of these names are based on an era or on slight differences in style or technique. Surprisingly, most art can be divided into three broad-based design styles:

- representational
- geometric
- nonobjective

There are definite differences between these design styles, so it is important to understand their characteristics and idiosyncrasies. The representational design style is so varied that it can be subdivided into six smaller categories or genres. The geometric design style is the most popular one for quilt-makers. The nonobjective design style is a huge category that is amazingly varied. Organic shapes can be used to help represent something or they can be nonobjective. Therefore, they are well suited to either category. Explore these different design styles and their subdivisions to find the ones that most closely relate to your creative personality and inquisitiveness.

DESIGN STYLE 1: REPRESENTATIONAL

Most artwork that represents nature or man-made objects is part of the broad-based *representational design style*. Because artistic expression is so varied in this category, it can be divided into six manageable divisions:

- *Realism* or *realistic*—a design that appears very real; a design that is similar to a photograph in its clarity

- *Impressionistic*—a design that gives an impression rather than visual clarity

- *Abstract*—a design that has been abstracted in some manner, resulting in an allusion or obscure imagery

- *Surreal*—a design that is dreamlike, unbelievable, or realistically impossible

- *Fanciful/whimsical*—a design that has been interpreted in an imaginative, whimsical, light-hearted, charming manner

- *Cultural art (also known as primitive art)*—a design based on the life or culture of a people from a specific country, region, and/or culture

Realistic Designs

If you want to create realistic art, then work in a *realistic* representational style. If this is your preference, you must be accurate in your presentation of imagery. You cannot guess at your shapes. The shapes must be realistically representational. Since it's difficult to hold an accurate image of a scene or an object in your mind's eye, a camera or a collection of images is imperative when creating realistic art. Keep files of images for design reference. Allow yourself to use the techniques, tools, and materials that will provide realism. Don't allow unwritten rules, procedures, or convention to limit your ability to create the imagery that inspires you.

Amazing realistic artwork is included in this book, such as *Georgette Tulips*. Others include *The Calm after the Storm, Water Curtain with Orchids,* and *Mountain Chapel* (pages 6, 11, and 28). A few of these designs are so lifelike that they seem as if they must be photographs, but they are not. The realistic portrayal of the blue heron in the back-side detail view of *In Hiding* (page 66) is stunning.

GEORGETTE TULIPS by Amanda Richardson, Cornwall, England, 12″ × 12″, 2008

The tulips in *Georgette Tulips* appear as if we can touch them, they are so realistic. Even the lustrous effect on the tulips' petals seems life-like. The soft tinted hues present delicacy in this high-key design (see Working in High Value, page 57). Amanda used silk, polyester, acetate, and cotton in different weaves to create this realistic design. *Georgette Tulips* is in a 1:1 ratio (pages 77–81).

Photo by the artist

You might prefer to work in a slightly less pronounced form of realism than photographically perfect realism. If so, slightly lessen the strength of some or all of the lines and objects in order to soften the realism. *Rhododendrons over Water* is a great example of how art illustrates softened realism. Other great examples include *Sunrise over Tuscany, Winter Walk, Fragrant Memories,* and *Tidal Flat* (pages 18, 16, 93, and 104).

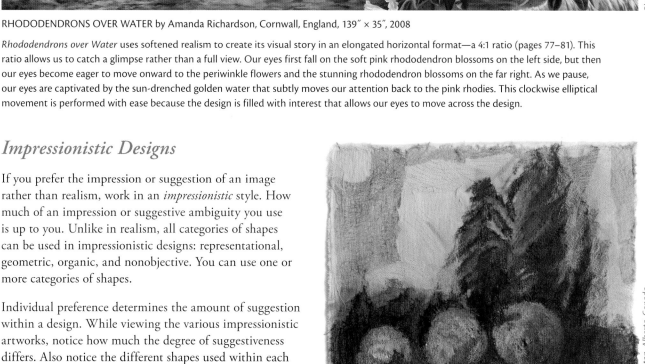

RHODODENDRONS OVER WATER by Amanda Richardson, Cornwall, England, 139″ × 35″, 2008

Photo by the artist

Rhododendrons over Water uses softened realism to create its visual story in an elongated horizontal format—a 4:1 ratio (pages 77–81). This ratio allows us to catch a glimpse rather than a full view. Our eyes first fall on the soft pink rhododendron blossoms on the left side, but then our eyes become eager to move onward to the periwinkle flowers and the stunning rhododendron blossoms on the far right. As we pause, our eyes are captivated by the sun-drenched golden water that subtly moves our attention back to the pink rhodies. This clockwise elliptical movement is performed with ease because the design is filled with interest that allows our eyes to move across the design.

Impressionistic Designs

If you prefer the impression or suggestion of an image rather than realism, work in an *impressionistic* style. How much of an impression or suggestive ambiguity you use is up to you. Unlike in realism, all categories of shapes can be used in impressionistic designs: representational, geometric, organic, and nonobjective. You can use one or more categories of shapes.

Individual preference determines the amount of suggestion within a design. While viewing the various impressionistic artworks, notice how much the degree of suggestiveness differs. Also notice the different shapes used within each design. To decrease realism and increase the idea of an impression, blur lines and use undefined, blurred textures.

Reflections is a good example of impressionism. A range of impressionism can be seen among *Five Apples, House through Arch, Marsh #18: Sunny Day, Dreaming of a Room of My Own, A City Walk in Spring,* and *Interwoven* (pages 7, 9, 18, 53, 84, and 116).

Photo by Seann Childs, Light Art Photography, Edmonton, Alberta, Canada

REFLECTIONS by Jayne Willoughby Scott, Edmonton, Alberta, Canada, 22″ × 30″, 2002

Reflections is a lovely example of an impressionistic scene. Impressionism, which is a genre that is part of the representational design style, offers visual suggestion rather than clarity. Most shapes are recognizable in this design, yet some are left to our imagination. This allows us a certain amount of visual interpretation.

Abstract Designs

Abstract designs are usually more ambiguous than impressionistic ones. They can be visually provocative brainteasers. Shapes from every category can be used to create abstract images. Images can be abstracted by being rearranged, reshaped, redesigned, partially hidden, or changed in some way. They can be skewed, stretched, compacted, or realigned. They can be cut apart, partially omitted, and repositioned.

When you create an abstract design, give your viewers enough visual clues to allow them to feel they can interpret your design. If they have no sense of what your design is about, it will leave them unsatisfied and uncomfortable. Think of your abstract design as a picture puzzle. Determine the degree of abstraction you want to provide and then decide how you will accomplish this. Use your imagination and have fun; there is no right or wrong in the matter.

Enjoy viewing the many wonderful abstract designs in this book, noting how each artist worked so imaginatively. For instance, *The Wedding Quilt* shows significant abstraction in its design, as it captivates our imagination. *Summer Rain* (page 86) is visually enthralling, as nonobjective shapes lead our eyes to see flowers in a garden. The flowers in *Floral Forms I* (page 87) have been re-formed to offer subtle visual intrigue. *Iris Beckoning* (page 52) offers a slightly different level of abstraction in its flower garden. *Setting Sun, Rising Moon* (page 102) provides realistic trees and moon but offers us an unexpected visual surprise with beautifully abstracted background elements. The trail of light surrounding the moon is quite abstracted in *Moon Dance* (page 113).

Surreal Designs

A design that is beyond reality is *surreal*. There may be parts of the design that appear realistic, but the overall imagery presents an unrealistic visual statement. Any category of shapes may be used in surreal designs. If you love the idea of creating impossible or improbable visions, or dreamlike imagery, let your imagination run wild. Surreal designs can be visually provocative and extremely interpretive, as in *It's About Time*. They are as varied as their creators. Surreal designs include *Dressed for the Party, Minor Miracle, Luminosity, Moonlight Sonata, A Dream of Swimming Points, In Hiding, Autumn Beauty, Kimberley Mystique,* and *Ogenblik (Twinkling of an Eye)* (pages 16, 31, 45, 49, 63, 66, 85, 92, and 98).

THE WEDDING QUILT by Jean Wells Keenan, Sisters, Oregon, 73″ × 63″, 2003

Jean combined geometric and representational shapes to create this fascinating abstract design. She chose the historic pattern New York Beauty as the purveyor of shapes. The abundant use of garden-theme and textural fabrics is perfect for this imaginary garden scene. This quilt, celebrating her son's and daughter's weddings, was inspired by Jean's garden and the beautiful scenery that surrounds it.

Photo by Valori Wells, Sisters, Oregon

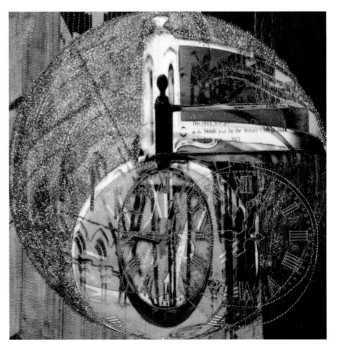

IT'S ABOUT TIME by Gloria Hansen, East Windsor, New Jersey, 10½″ × 10½″, 2008

It's About Time is an example of a design using representational and geometric shapes to create a surreal design—a design that is dreamlike, unreal, or impossible. Gloria created this artwork with sheer fabrics, digital imagery, pastels, and artist crayons.

Photo by the artist

Fanciful, Whimsical, or Charming Designs

If you like to create representational designs that are imaginative in nature, give your artistic license free rein. Choose any category of shapes that works with your design ideas; then play. *Footloose* is a fun-filled example of a fanciful or whimsical design, as are *Overrun, 5 of Clubs, Dresden Flower Garden, Friends in High Places, Fall, Snail Mail, Good Old Mountain Music Memories,* and *Birdland* (pages 74, 89, 111, 122, 136, 137, and 139).

FOOTLOOSE by Rachel Wetzler, St. Charles, Illinois, 42″ × 38″, 2006

Marvelously whimsical, *Footloose* falls into the fanciful genre that makes up a small part of the representational design style. You can't help smiling when you see this artwork. Rachel uses repetition of shapes to create great unity. Her use of contrast is delightful (the shoes, of course!).

Photo by the artist

Cultural Art

Cultural art can include designs that tell a visual story based on the life or traditions of a people from a specific country, region, and/or culture. Many people refer to this type of art as primitive. *Playing Soccer* tells a visual story about life in a South African village. The design is beautifully embroidered by a woman who belongs to a needlework group that creates art pieces to sell to support the members' families and their village. The detail in this design is considerable and the workmanship superb. Also, cultural art can include designs that are reminiscent of a specific historic period within a region, country, or culture. For example, *Jessica's Flower Basket* (page 109) is reminiscent of early Americana appliqué quilts. It is a contemporary design based on a historic style of quilting in America's early years.

PLAYING SOCCER by Rosinah Mabasa, Winterveld, South Africa, 24″ × 24″

Playing Soccer is an example of cultural art—art that represents life within one's culture. This hand-embroidered storytelling artwork illustrates the concept that design is a universal language of visual storytelling. This artist is a member of the Mapula Embroidery Project, an embroidery group that generates income to support the members' families through embroidery.

DESIGN STYLE 2: GEOMETRIC

The *geometric design style* is as varied as the shapes are. Quiltmakers are renowned for their geometric designs. If you are a beginning quilter or an artist from another medium, you can find hundreds of historic quilt blocks in many quilt-block pattern books. *The Ultimate Pineapple* and *LeMoyne Star & Friends* (pages 126 and 135) are examples of quilts using historic blocks in a traditional manner. You can use historic blocks as a jumping-off point to make your own designs by adding or deleting lines and shapes, manipulating colors, changing values, or using the shapes innovatively.

Original designs based on historic block patterns are many in this book. One good example is *Moonsnail.* Other examples are *I've Been to Mecca, Northern Lights, Fantasia, Memories of Monet, Sedona, The Colour of Jazz, Pineapple Surprise Again, Perspectives II,* and *Unnamed Log Cabin* (pages 7, 20, 45, 54, 59, 61, 108, and 126). In some designs, the traditional roots can be seen at first glance; however, a few take a bit of studying before one sees the traditional connection.

If you love geometric shapes, then it should be quite exciting for you to make your own geometric designs from scratch. The options are unending. Colors, values, shapes, and designs are highly personal. As you browse through this book, notice how the different geometric shapes are used to create designs. One example is *Bali Wedding Star.* A varied selection includes *Tropical Radiance, Baskets & Blossoms, Thistle Pods, Ticonderoga Star, Infinity, Jewel's Garden,* and *Bear Tracks in the Garden* (pages 10, 57, 59, 78, 85, 133, and 135).

BALI WEDDING STAR by Judy and Brad Niemeyer, Kalispell, Montana, 80″ × 80″, 2009

Bali Wedding Star is aptly named, as circles and stars seemingly embrace to form a beautiful union. The interaction between stars and circles enhances the geometric design and creates movement. This softly toned star quilt was paper pieced using Hoffman California Bali Batiks. (Pattern is available.)

Photo by Judy Niemeyer Quilting

MOONSNAIL by Meredith Annett, Halifax, Nova Scotia, Canada, 48″ × 63″, 1997

Meredith used geometric shapes from a historic pattern to create the structure for this design. She then chose value as her featured element and allowed colors and values to shift ingeniously from top to bottom. This quilt uses over 900 different fabrics and contains over 8,000 pieces.

Photo by Chris Reardon, Halifax, Nova Scotia, Canada

Explore the possibility of working with kaleidoscopes as in *Cheddar Cheese* (page 21); tessellations as in *Colour of Jazz* (page 61); concentric circles as in *Amazon Star* (page 58) and *Primrose* (below); and elliptical designs as in *Tsunami* (page 23). Consider designing with fractals, spirals, or sequences as in *Fibonacci's Garden* (page 76).

Don't be afraid to think creatively. Figure out different ways to use geometric shapes to create innovative designs. *It's About Time* (page 61) is an excellent example of using simple geometric shapes to create beautiful contemporary art. Other innovative examples created with geometric shapes include *House through Arch, Boxing Out, Thunderclouds Approaching, Overlay IV: Jungle Light, Galaxy,* and *Floating Frames* (pages 9, 90, 91, 93, 99, and 100). Another example is *Don't Bug Me. Big Bang + 1 Second* (page 94) is an amazing design that incorporates intricately pieced multicolored shapes, producing an explosion of color throughout the design surface while also providing a luminous diagonal line.

PRIMROSE by Anna Faustino, Tobyhanna, Pennsylvania, 50½″ × 50″, 2006

A magnificent geometric design using concentric circles and radial symmetry, this artwork beckons our eyes to its center and then urges movement outward through the use of line and reiterating shapes. Color, shape, value, line, texture, scale, and proportion all play a role in this design's visual success.

Photo by the artist

DON'T BUG ME by Anna Faustino, Tobyhanna, Pennsylvania, 44½″ × 48¼″, 2006

Anna created a wonderfully exuberant bilateral design using color, value, and shape as the primary movers in this artwork. Notice how visually effective it is to have the geometric shapes become smaller as they move toward the design's center. This design uses a primary triadic color plan, which provides its happy spirit.

Photo by the artist

DESIGN STYLE 3: NONOBJECTIVE

The *nonobjective design style* is noninterpretive—the art does not represent any idea or object. The beauty of this design style is in the way the artist creates a visual symphony of color, value, line, texture, direction, and shape. This design style lets a viewer's imagination engage in provocative interaction with a design. Sometimes an artwork's title provides a clue as to how the artist wants you to interpret a design, but most often the interpretation is left to the viewer.

With the exception of representational shapes, nonobjective designs can be created from all categories of shapes. Balance plays an important role; most designs are asymmetrical. For this reason, nonobjective art is best explored when you've had previous design experience. *Cellular Structure VIII (Oval Shift)* (page 31) is a beautiful example of nonobjective art using nonobjective shapes. *Midnight Fantasy #6* (page 22) is a nonobjective design combining organic and geometric shapes. The organic curves play the dominant role while the geometric shapes provide contrast and additional interest. See *Layers of Time* for a nonobjective design. Other wonderful nonobjective designs include *Fandango, Nest III, Dream of Infinity,* and *California Reel* (pages 87, 101, 103, and 132).

A Closing Thought

Creating is not a static endeavor. The design style that excited you a few years ago may not be the one that your creative soul yearns for now. If you find yourself struggling to create, be open to the idea that your creative spirit might want to change course and explore another avenue. It takes courage to stop what you are doing, reassess, and move toward an unfamiliar pathway. Don't let anyone talk you out of moving out of your comfort zone when you know it's time to make a change. No one else knows better than you what your creative spirit needs in order to interpret your unique visual stories. If you allow yourself to be curious and imaginative, and then give yourself time to explore possibilities, amazing designs will evolve.

LAYERS OF TIME by Sylvia Naylor, Cambridge, Ontario, Canada, 23″ × 35″, 2008

Layers of Time uses nonobjective shapes to create a sense of timelessness in this evocative design. Quietly dramatic in its wintry hues, its beauty is created by the featuring of high-value toned hues in a horizontal focus structure. The softly colored, richly textured horizontal shapes are quite fascinating as the layers subtly shift and change in their upward progression.

Photo by the artist

ACTIVITIES AND EXERCISES

1. Visit museums, galleries, and art/craft shows, and look at art books. Note what design styles and shapes you are most and least drawn to. You may be surprised to find that the shapes and style you are currently using in your work are not those that excite you or those that truly reflect your design personality.

2. To experiment with the representational design style (page 32), first look through this book to view the representational designs. Next, select your own photo image to use for this activity. Enlarge the image to a workable size. Make six to eight copies. Then do each of the following exercises. If one of these designs especially excites you, begin thinking about how you might work with this type of design. Begin playing with ideas. Start an idea file.

a. Think about how you can create an impressionistic image. Be imaginative. You might start by cutting the design apart and putting it back together again, so it appears as an impression. You can use one of your extra copies to help create an impression by overlaying some areas. You can use paint, colored pencils, chalk, or other means to help create your impressionistic imagery.

b. Create an abstract version of your photo image. Using one or more copies of the image, cut or break apart the image, as if it were a puzzle. You can cut it into strips, geometric shapes, organic curves, nonobjective shapes, or a combination of these. Then create a design, playing abstractly with the pieces.

c. Create a surreal design, adding a few other photos or images to your original image. Find ways to make your design fascinatingly unrealistic. Be imaginative.

d. Create a whimsical design by adding other elements. Cut and paste, paint, color, and so on. Let your imagination play. Have fun. If another idea pops into your mind as you are working, make a second whimsical design using another copy of your image.

3. If you love working with geometric shapes, expand your knowledge of art and geometry. Study the works of Wassily Kandinsky, Leonardo Fibonacci, M.C. Escher, and others who have used geometry in their art. Take notes of the ideas that interest you. Consider doing one or more of the following.

a. Research the Fibonacci number sequence (page 76). Explore this relationship with shells, flowers, petals, seed heads, and so on. Create at least one design using the Fibonacci sequence.

b. Research Fibonacci spirals. Play with this concept. Then create a design using Fibonacci spirals.

c. Research Clifford circle chains. If you like these circle chains and find the method for creating them fascinating, then select one of the Clifford circle chains to use in creating your own design.

4. Explore the design possibilities with knots, fractals, rotational patterning, and cubic patterning. Use library books or online searches to see the many design opportunities using these geometric designs. Select your favorite option to create a new design.

5. To create nonobjective designs, begin by creating mini designs on index cards. Use fabric, colored paper, paint, colored pencils, or any other materials for these designs. Create at least one design each day (number or date each card on the back side, so you can keep the cards in sequential order). After a month's time, place your design cards, in order, on a design wall or similar space. What do you notice? How have you improved? Do you see frequent similarities? What are your strengths? Do you have areas to improve? If so, what are they? Take notes on everything you have discovered. Keep these design cards. Continue doing at least one design a day for another month. If you are particularly enamored with one design or portions of a design, put it in a "favorites" file for future use.

6. Play with organic shapes. Start collecting photos, advertisements, or online images of organic shapes. Doodle while watching television or talking on the telephone. Place these in a file labeled "organic" and use them for inspiration and reference for future projects.

CHAPTER FOUR

COLOR
Visually Enticing Flavors

The most visible element in a design is usually color. It is often the element that takes on the leading role. It is versatile and amenable. Color can create a mood; be comfortable in any season; show energy; promote mellowness, freshness, or calmness; give you the approximate time of day; and evoke myriad emotions and thoughts. It can be dramatic or subtle. It is very responsive to your creative desires—as long as you have some basic understanding of its character, its compatibility, and its idiosyncrasies. Although color can be a lifetime subject of study and deserves its own book, you should have enough color information after reading this chapter to create beautiful, if not stunning, designs.

Color—Personality Plus

We are affected by the colors that surround us in our homes and workplaces. Color can affect our mood, our productivity, and the amount of food we consume. Color responses can be cultural and emotional. Other responses are physical, due to electrical impulses sent by the eye's retina to the hypothalamus, which controls appetite, metabolism, and behavior. Knowing a color's characteristics, limitations, and physical effects can help you create the best design possible for your purpose. Here is a glimpse into the most influential color personalities that surround us daily.

BLUE

The most beloved color in the world is blue. Because the blue of sky and water is calming, this color creates a sense of tranquility in our brains. Blue is gender neutral. Deep cool blue hues appear to clear the mind, while light blues calm the mind. The cooler the blue, the more soothing it is. It is an intellectual color, as well as one that conveys logic, trustworthiness, and idealism. Blue rooms are considered productive. Blue is rarely seen in nature except in sky and water. Coldness can be associated with blue, so be cautious about using icy blues or strongly grayed blues as the major colors in homes, offices, and art in the far north. Warm blues such as aqua blue elicit a more playful mood than cooler blues.

GREEN

Green, the most prevalent color in nature, represents the earth, nature, and the revival of spring. It symbolizes rebirth, fertility, youth, peace, and harmony. Because of its middle placement in the light-wave spectrum, it provides natural balance. Green physically relaxes the eye and has a calming effect on people. Green is the most popular decorating color because of its restfulness. However, chartreuse and yellow-green have too much yellow in their makeup to be calming; they are stimulating. If you want a restful green, stay with a cool, balanced green.

YELLOW

Yellow is the most exciting, cheerful, and spirited of all colors. It exudes optimism, confidence, high self-esteem, happiness, hope, and friendliness. Being the strongest color, yellow is psychologically stimulating and emotional. Yellow is an extrovert's color. In its purest form, a small splash of yellow attracts great attention. It is the most difficult color for the eye to absorb. It increases the metabolism and can overwhelm us physically when we are surrounded by it. People lose their tempers more often in yellow rooms. If yellow is your featured color, use its purest form judiciously. For less intensity, substitute whitened, blackened, or grayed hues for the pure color. Blackened yellows turn into beautiful shades of olive.

RED

Red symbolizes life's blood and vibrancy. Its warmth quickly attracts attention. Red evokes many emotions. It's impulsive, lively, passionate, energetic, and powerful. It exudes a feeling of warmth, heat, fire, and excitement. Red hints of love and sex. It evokes courage. Besides bringing out strong emotions, red causes strong physical changes in the body. This may be due to red having the longest visible wavelength. Red increases the viewer's breathing rate and can stimulate the heart to beat faster. It also stimulates the nervous system, raises the pulse rate, and increases body tension. Red tends to stimulate the appetite, so many restaurants use red as a decorating color. Red's physical changes can make people more aggressive, demanding, defiant, and angry. Most people cannot be surrounded by red for a long time. Take care when using red in visual arts or interior design. Instead of using its purest form, consider using derivative forms of red. When red is whitened, luscious corals are created. If it is blackened, beautiful reddish rusts and browns as well as maroons are created. When red is muted, the strong reactions to red are diminished.

ORANGE

Orange is a stimulating, flamboyant, energetic color. It is warm and playful. It elicits the strongest emotional reaction of any color in its purest form—you either love it or hate it. Orange is a difficult color to ignore. It demands attention. Physically, orange brings about a dual reaction in people. First, it stimulates the appetite. Second, it is a color that is difficult to be surrounded by for more than a short period. Consequently, orange is a perfect decorating color for fast-food restaurants. Orange can create aggressiveness and overemotional reactions. A little bit of pure orange can go a long way in both interior design and art. When orange is diluted with white, beautiful apricot hues are created. When black is added, warm, luscious rusts and browns are created. These hues modify the boldness of orange and make it less emotional or reactive.

VIOLET

Historically, violet has been considered the color of royalty, spirituality, wealth, and nobility. Violet was the first dye ever made. Because it was so rare and costly to create, violet was reserved for royalty. It was against the law for others to wear violet. Because of its origin, violet has a regal, luxurious quality associated with it. Violet is the darkest pure color and is made from the shortest light wave discernable to the naked eye. A violet that appears bluish is a color called blue-violet. A violet that appears warm is called red-violet.

Because of violet's historic importance, it has long been associated with wisdom, truth, enlightenment, creativity, prestige, importance, and high birth. It is an uplifting color. It is thought to evoke introspection and contemplation. Many religious or educational robes are violet or adorned with violet. Additionally, violet has been used as a mourning color.

BROWN

Brown is not a pure color, so it is not on the color wheel. It is created when black is added to warm colors, such as red, orange-red, red-orange, orange, yellow-orange, and orange-yellow. A brown made from red is a reddish brown; a brown made from orange is a rusty brown; a brown made from orange-yellow is a warm yellowish brown. The more black that is added, the darker the brown. If it's been slightly grayed, the brown will appear softly muted. Brown's earthiness makes it a naturally comfortable color for most people. Brown exudes the feeling of simplicity, endurance, stability, home, and nature. Brown is a favorite color of many men. Negative feelings become associated with brown when too much gray is added to it, as then it can appear drab, dirty, or dull.

BLACK

Black is created when color is totally absorbed; it is the absence of light. It is a serious, solemn hue that exudes no frivolity. In the fashion world, black is timeless, sophisticated, glamorous, and very stylish. Black is thought to be the color of night. It is the color most associated with the unknown and mystery. Black can convey emptiness and darkness. For centuries it has been associated with sadness, fear, death, and mourning.

Black is an excellent neutral for intense, brilliant colors and rich shades. It can be overpowering and too heavy to partner with some hues. For instance, black can overwhelm delicate tints, such as apricot, pink, mint green, lavender, and light blue. It can make toned (grayed) colors look drab. If you're going to use black with toned hues, don't let it overpower them. Use black in your design with care. For instance, use it to make brilliant colors more stunning and for vibrant contrast. Strong, vibrant black is rarely seen in nature. If you are using it in a nature scene, consider softening it to a charcoal, so that it doesn't overwhelm the other hues.

GRAY

Psychologically, gray is a neutral hue. It exudes feelings of respect and reverence. It is quiet and subtle. At times it is considered elegant. Gray conveys wisdom, conservatism, modesty, and reliability. When a color is slightly grayed, it becomes muted or visually softened. As more gray is added, a color becomes more subtle. If the color is saturated with gray, it will appear as gray with a hint of the color (such as blued gray or pinkish gray). Gray is an excellent neutral hue when working with toned (grayed) or muted hues. The most beautiful tones are created by mixing a color with its complement, rather than adding a neutral gray or a black/white mixture.

WHITE

White is the opposite of black. It is created when all color is reflected. Although it gives a spacious feeling, it can be difficult for the eye to absorb, thereby causing eyestrain. It's uncompromising. White symbolizes purity, cleanliness, sterility, innocence, truth, hope, simplicity, and sophistication. It's considered a sacred color. Physically, the color white affects us by helping clarify our minds. There are numerous hues of white, moving from soft, warm white to cool, blue white. Too much white, or white in the wrong setting, can convey coldness, sterility, unfriendliness, and unimaginativeness. Pure white is rarely present in nature.

Color—Nature's Way

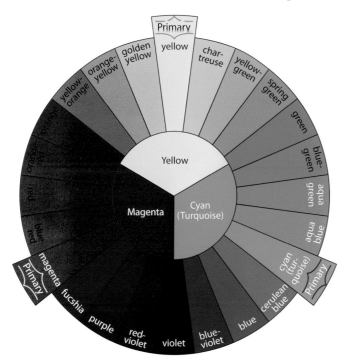

The Ives color wheel reflects the colors in our world and gives us nature's most beautiful color partnerships.

The most glorious hues and color combinations in the world are created from the color wheel based on nature and the light wave. This color wheel, also known as the Ives color wheel, creates its dynamic pure colors with yellow, magenta, and cyan (turquoise) as its primaries. The Ives color wheel reflects the colors in our world and gives us nature's most beautiful color partnerships. The CMYK color system is based on this color wheel.

Almost all of us grew up with the color wheel that uses yellow, red, and blue as its primaries. This color wheel was developed over a hundred years ago by artisans. Advances in the physics of color that we have available to us now show that this older color wheel, although comfortable because we're used to it, does not give accurate color information with regard to color relationships and plans. If you are still using the older artisan's color wheel, seriously consider replacing it with this scientifically accurate one. Then you can be certain that your color combinations are natural and accurate and provide the most beautiful effects.

NATURE—THE SUPREME COLOR ORGANIZER

Every color in the world can be placed into one of four groups: pure, tint, shade, or tone. Each of these groups is called a *color scale*. Each color scale has its own personality and use in design. When you create a design, you can use one or more color scales, but one should play the dominant role. Feature the color scale that best suits your design intentions. The characteristics of and differences between the four color scales are listed below.

Pure colors include the primary colors and all colors that have been created by blending any two primary colors. The most common pure colors can be found on the Ives color wheel. These colors are pure because they have not been diluted in any way. They are at their most intense state. They are as brilliant as they can possibly be. Pure colors are used for dramatic effects, summer imagery, and attention-getting accents. As you gaze at the designs in this book, you will see splashes of pure colors added to many, with good effect. It is far better to excite us with a small amount of pure color than to overwhelm our senses with an entire design of it. The pure color scale is the dominant scale in *Pizzazz*, which is a visual celebration of winter's dramatic sunsets.

PIZZAZZ by Joen Wolfrom, Fox Island, Washington, 66″ × 66″, 2003

The colors in *Pizzazz* move from yellow to violet by way of bridging (see Principle 7: Bridging, page 103). Half of the color wheel is used for this analogous coloring, which is the maximum range for this color plan. (Pattern is available.)

Photo by Ken Wagner, Seattle, Washington

Tints are hues created when white is added to a pure color. They range from blush white to a hue just slightly lighter than the pure color. Tints include apricot, pink, lavender, mint green, light blue, and robin's egg blue. Soft tints bring a delicate feeling to a design. These hues tend to represent spring.

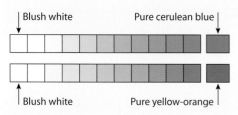

Two tint scales: White is added to pure cerulean blue and yellow-orange to create a selection of tints.

Springtime in the Valley uses the tint scale as its dominant scale in this sunrise scene of Mount Rainier overlooking the tulip fields. Using the tint scale brings a delicate uplifting feeling to the scene.

SPRINGTIME IN THE VALLEY by Joen Wolfrom, Fox Island, Washington, 156" × 54", 1986

To create the illusion of a sunrise, I surrounded the sky's soft, clear yellow hues with slightly toned hues in the sky and mountain range. As a result, clear colors appear luminous against the toned hues. Depth is created through the use of atmospheric perspective: each land element in this scene's background becomes lighter in value, grayer in coloring, and less distinct in detail as it recedes into the distance. The amount of change from one element to the other dictates how close or how far the elements appear from each other. The hills behind the bulb fields are far from Mount Rainier, the mountain range, and its foothills, as their dark hues indicate. We can tell that the foothills and mountain range are near in distance to each other because the value and tonality of the two are very similar.

Photo by Ken Wagner, Seattle, Washington

What Is a Color Family?

The *head* of each color family is a pure color. (The 24 major pure colors are shown on the Ives color wheel on page 43.) Each color family is comprised of its pure color and all the hues that can be created from it. This includes all whitened (tinted) and blackened (shaded) hues and the multitude of colors created through the graying (toning) of these hues.

Each pure color has its own set of tints, shades, and tones to make up the hues in its family. For example, the violet color family includes pure violet along with scores of lavenders (tints), dark and deep violets (shades), and hundreds of toned hues for the entire range of violet from blush lavender to its deepest violet.

Shades are hues created when black is added to a pure color. They range from a hue just slightly darker than the pure color to almost black. Dark shades are luscious and rich looking.

Pure
cerulean blue   Cerulean blue shades

Pure
yellow-orange   Yellow-orange shades

Two shade scales: Black has been added to pure cerulean blue and yellow-orange to create a selection of shades.

Blackened hues include avocado, olive, rust, brown, cranberry, maroon, navy, ink navy, emerald green, teal, dark violet, and deep purple. A color name that includes *dark* or *deep* connotes a shade. Rich warm shades are the hues of autumn. Cool shades represent night, deep forests, and rich elegance. The darkest hues in *Fantasia* are shades. *Northern Lights* (page 110) uses the shade scale predominantly for its design. The trees in *Luminosity* are richly shaded. *Nostalgia* (page 65) uses several shaded hues in its coloring.

LUMINOSITY by Kay D. Haerland, Green Point, New South Wales, Australia, 41½″ × 30″, 2008

Luminosity is a powerful design filled with many interesting features. Kay has created great drama through the illusion of luminosity. By surrounding the vibrant yellow hues with softly toned green colors, she has made the ground glow with luminosity. Visual drama is further increased by the addition of the darkened trees standing in powerful unity, created with deeply shaded browns. A small figure is standing at the base of the largest tree, providing not only intrigue but a visual gauge as to the tree's immenseness. In this asymmetrical design, Kay has provided visual balance through the placement of trees, the darkened forest floor, and the luminous area.

FANTASIA by Joen Wolfrom, Fox Island, Washington, 77″ × 77″, 2007

Fantasia, an original offset Log Cabin design, illustrates dimensionality through the use of atmospheric perspective. This design's two layers are clearly visible because the background is more toned (grayer), lighter in value, and less distinct in detail than the foreground. The darkest hues in *Fantasia* are shades of green and red-violet. The soft luster seen in the red-violet and green hues is created through subtle value change. (Pattern is available.)

Tones are hues created when a pure color, tint, or shade has been grayed in some manner. If the graying is minimal, the intensity of the color is slightly softened. If the toning is extreme, the color appears gray with a hint of the original color. Tones include beige, tan, rose, mauve, taupe, heather, plum, dusty teal, salmon, and some navy hues. Subtle tones create calmness. They evoke the feelings of winter.

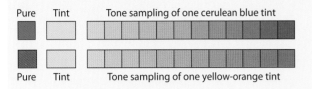

Two tone scales: Gray has been added to a tint of cerulean blue and yellow-orange to create a range of tones.

Most art includes some use of tones. Every artwork in this chapter uses tones to varying degrees. *Pinwheel Evolution (YoYo 9)* and *Lavandula* each show a beautiful blend of toned hues that vary in intensity. *Blue Ginkgoes* (page 48) is another excellent example of the wonderful use of tones. The more subdued the artwork, the more the colors have been toned.

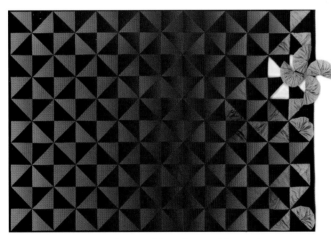

PINWHEEL EVOLUTION (YOYO 9) by Helen Remick, Seattle, Washington, 56″ × 40″, 2010

Pinwheel Evolution (YoYo 9) illustrates beautifully how a complementary color scheme can be quietly dramatic with softly toned hues. This quilt's color play is superbly executed with the use of value change. For contrast and interest, extra texture has been created in some of the pinwheels.

Photo by Mark Frey, Yelm, Washington

LAVANDULA by Wil Fritsma, Luchtenburg, the Netherlands, 42½″ × 49¼″, 2009

Wil created a beautifully subtle design through her use of toned hues. *Lavandula* incorporates a narrow range of analogous colors in its split-complementary color plan. The subtle contrasting warm yellow-green hues flitter throughout, bringing a rich sparkle to the design. Wil used photo imagery as the primary feature in her design.

Photo by the artist

COMBINING THE COLOR SCALES TO CREATE STUNNING DESIGNS

Designs that use only the pure scale can be too strong for most settings. The eye cannot absorb such strong coloration for a long duration. If you want your design to be soft and delicate, you may choose to use only tints. If you want your design to be softly muted, you may choose to work only with the tone scale. More than likely you will choose to work with two or more color scales because the subtle variations in color scale will help you to create focus and interest. You can see a variation of color scale use in each artwork within this chapter. Look through the gallery pages to study the color scale use in the artworks you particularly like, in order to see if there is a color-scale-use correlation. Use the color scale or color scale combinations that seem most comfortable for you. There is no one right way to work.

Nature's Most Beautiful Color Plans

Nature's sense of color is phenomenal, so using her as your guide is a solid plan for success. Below is an overview of nature's five major color plans.

MONOCHROMATIC COLOR PLAN

A *monochromatic color plan* uses only one *color family.* Its beauty is created through value and/or intensity change. A sample of a *value range,* which moves colors from light to dark, can be seen below. An example of a monochromatic color plan using an *intensity range,* changing the color's amount of grayness, follows.

A monochromatic plan can be very sophisticated. It is most beautiful when a wide range of value or intensity steps are used—at least seven value or intensity steps. If you use fewer than seven steps, space the value or intensity range evenly, so the hues move fully from light to dark. Artwork using the monochromatic color plan is uncommon, but this color plan is often seen in nature. The summer evening scene below reflects a calming monochromatic plan.

Pure   Full value range of orange-red with tints, pure hue, and shades

Monochromatic color plan using value changes of orange-red

Selected tones of a tint from orange-red

Monochromatic color plan using intensity changes of an orange-red tint

This summer evening scene illustrates a blue monochromatic color plan.

COMPLEMENTARY COLOR PLAN

A complementary color scheme uses colors that lie directly across from each other on the color wheel. An example of complementary partners is orange-red and aqua blue.

Complementary color plan: orange-red and aqua blue

If you have not used the scientifically accurate color wheel (page 43) previously, you will want to become familiar with nature's complementary partners. There is an amazing difference in beauty between the complements on the historic color wheel and the complements based on the natural physics of light. The true complements are glorious together. Nature's complementary color partners are as follows:

- Yellow and violet
- Chartreuse and red-violet
- Yellow-green and purple
- Spring green and fuchsia
- Green and magenta
- Blue-green and blue-red
- Aqua green and red
- Aqua blue and orange-red
- Turquoise and orange
- Cerulean blue and yellow-orange
- Blue and orange-yellow
- Blue-violet and golden yellow

Complementary color schemes are often dramatic, but they can be soft and subtle. The background hues in *Blue Ginkgoes* complement the flowers perfectly. *Pinwheel Evolution (YoYo 9)* (page 46) uses the partnership of spring green and fuchsia.

BLUE GINKGOES by Norma Schlager, Danbury, Connecticut, 20″ × 25″, 2005

The use of complementary colors in *Blue Ginkgoes* brings natural harmony to this design. The uneven number of leaves promotes visual balance. Beauty is further enhanced because the darkest element (the largest leaf) is placed near the bottom of the design. Overlapping was used to enhance dimensionality. Norma used her own hand-dyed fabrics to create *Blue Ginkgoes*. The great textural effects were created with extensive free-motion quilting using variegated rayon thread.

You can use a pure color, along with any of its tints, shades, and tones, or you can omit the pure color if you want a less dramatic impact. Have one complementary color family play the dominant role in the design; the other has a secondary role. If the two colors are of equal visual importance, our eyes will flit back and forth between colors because they won't know where to rest. This results in visual discomfort.

ANALOGOUS COLOR PLAN

An *analogous color plan* combines colors that lie next to each other on the color wheel with a usual range of three to seven color families.

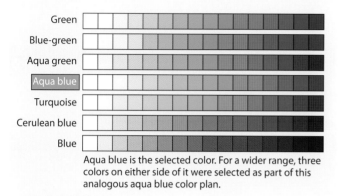

Green
Blue-green
Aqua green
Aqua blue
Turquoise
Cerulean blue
Blue

Aqua blue is the selected color. For a wider range, three colors on either side of it were selected as part of this analogous aqua blue color plan.

Analogous color plan using aqua blue as the selected color

If you use a greater expansion than shown, limit yourself to no more than half the color wheel and use an uneven number of colors. You can work with a harmonious color-wash blend of hues in the range or select dominant, secondary, and accent colors. Artwork using analogous color plans in this chapter includes *Pizzazz* and *Memories of Monet* (pages 43 and 54). There are many analogously colored designs in this book, including *Tropical Radiance, Water Curtain with Orchids, Autumn Walk, A Dream of Swimming Points, Infinity,* and *Overlay IV: Jungle Light* (pages 10, 11, 63, 85, and 93).

MOONLIGHT SONATA by Barbara Shapel, Washougal, Washington, 39" × 63", 2007

The quiet beauty in this design is created by the softly toned analogous hues that lie side by side on the color wheel. This creates visual harmony. The herons' beaks provide a warm contrast, creating an analogous variation based on realism. *Moonlight Sonata* uses a triangular structure for balance, with the moon being the apex, and the bottom lily pad and stones being the other two points. The herons lead our eyes right to the moon with the diagonal line. The bright grass provides an additional anchor of interest and visual weight.

Photo by Mark Frey, Yelm, Washington

SPLIT-COMPLEMENTARY COLOR PLAN

The *split-complementary color plan* combines the analogous and complementary color plans to create something new. The beauty of this color plan is its natural temperature shift, due to the complement. Most commonly, a range of three or five analogous colors combine with the middle color's complement.

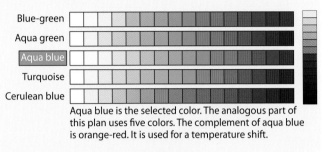

Aqua blue is the selected color. The analogous part of this plan uses five colors. The complement of aqua blue is orange-red. It is used for a temperature shift.

Split-complementary color plan using aqua blue as the selected color

A working strategy is to select one color to take the dominant role, another to play the secondary role, and the rest to take minor positions. It can be quite stunning to have the complementary hue be used as the dominant color. *Lavandula* (page 46) is enhanced beautifully with glimpses of yellow-green shimmering throughout its analogous hues from the other side of the color wheel. *Plait* also uses a split-complementary plan. You can see how effectively this plan's temperature shift enhances a design.

PLAIT by Lies Bos-Varkevisser, Enschede, the Netherlands, 62″ × 90″, 2007

Plait uses the split-complementary color plan to provide the warm color contrast amid the cool blues and greens. Lies used a wide value range of contrasting warm reds, bringing added interest to this quilt.

Photo by the artist

If you extend the analogous range to seven colors, you might consider increasing the complementary contrast to the complement and one neighboring color on each side of it. This addition can lead to subtle color vibration on the complementary side. This extended plan can be extraordinarily beautiful.

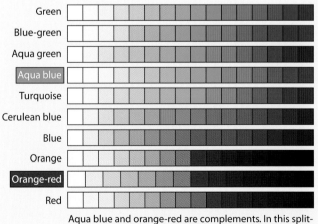

Aqua blue and orange-red are complements. In this split-complementary plan, the analogous part uses seven colors with aqua blue in the center. To create color vibration, orange-red is accompanied by its two neighboring colors for the temperature shift.

Split-complementary expanded color plan

TRIADIC COLOR PLAN

Seldom seen in the north, this color plan is reflected in many gorgeous tropical flowers and birds. The *triadic color plan* uses three colors that are an equal distance from each other on the color wheel. On a 24-step color wheel, the triadic combinations are as follows:

- Yellow, cyan (turquoise), magenta
- Chartreuse, cerulean blue, blue-red
- Yellow-green, blue, red
- Spring green, blue-violet, orange-red
- Green, violet, orange
- Blue-green, red-violet, yellow-orange
- Aqua green, purple, orange-yellow
- Aqua blue, fuchsia, golden yellow

Most designers who use the triadic color plan use the primary triad of yellow, cyan (turquoise), and magenta. However, every triadic combination can be quite stunning. Orange-red, spring green, and blue-violet are beautiful triadic partners.

BALI GEESE by Cindy L. Kurey, Albuquerque, New Mexico, 56″ × 65″, 2008

Using the primary triadic color plan, *Bali Geese* illustrates excellent use of the entire range of colors and values within a design. Using 224 batik fabrics, this quilt shows outstanding repetition and unity. Variety is provided by the changing direction of the geese and the colors. *Bali Geese* was adapted from Something Scrappy, an original pattern by Nann Blaine Hilyard, which was featured in the November 2005 issue of *The Quilter Magazine*.

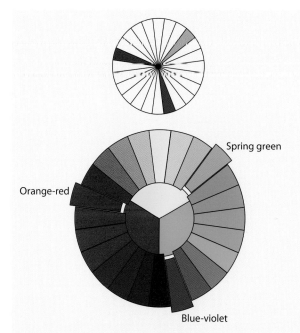

Triadic color plan partners orange-red, spring green, and blue-violet

In a triadic plan, choose one color family to be dominant, another to take the secondary role, and the third to play a minor role, or use the total blending of the hues to make a harmonic design. Use as many members of each of the three color families in your design as you wish. To enhance the beauty of this design, blend each of the triadic colors with its partners. The result is beautiful intermingling hues. An example of a triadic blending of the partners is shown below.

The triadic colors can be blended to create additional hues for a triadic color plan. Here you can see the mixing between orange-red and spring green, orange-red and blue-violet, and spring green and blue-violet.

Mixing triadic partners

When you blend yellow, turquoise, and magenta together, you get the colors of the color wheel. Therefore, when you see an artwork that uses almost every color under the sun, you can be certain it is made from a primary triadic color plan, as in *Bali Geese*. If you use this triad, use the entire spectrum of the color wheel—don't leave one color section out, as it will look incomplete. The primary triadic plan was used in many designs, including *House through Arch, Midnight Fantasy #6, Cellular Structure VIII (Oval Shift)*, and *Don't Bug Me* (pages 9, 22, 31, and 37).

Enhancing Your Design with Dimension

The warmer and more intense a color is, the more it will advance in your design. Use color temperature to help create the illusion of depth, particularly when your design features a close-in view, as does *Iris Beckoning*.

IRIS BECKONING by Joen Wolfrom, Fox Island, Washington, 40″ × 60″, 1996

In this abstract garden design, *Iris Beckoning* illustrates the concept of color temperature promoting a sense of depth. The warm iris colors advance in this design while the cooler vegetation hues recede into the background. This is set in a 2:3 ratio (pages 77–81).

Photo by Ken Wagner, Seattle, Washington

Color temperature is relative. You can make almost any color appear warm or cool. The closer a color is to yellow, the warmer its temperature; the farther away a color is from yellow, the cooler the color (see the Ives color wheel, page 43). If you want one color to appear warm, place it next to a cooler color. You can make the same color appear cool by placing it next to a warmer color. For example, green will appear warm next to a blue and cool when placed next to chartreuse.

Color temperature is relative.

There will be times when you won't want a warm color to advance or a cool color to recede. When that's the case, you have to cleverly conspire against color's natural temperature tendencies by changing the intensity of the color. You have to make the color either more or less intense. If you want a warm color to recede into the background, lessen its intensity or its brilliance by making it more toned (grayed). You may also need to lighten or blacken the color as you gray it. However, the more a color is grayed, the more it will recede. To make a cool color advance, increase its purity; make it more brilliant.

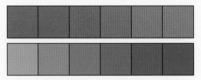

If you want a cool color to advance and a warm color to recede, change the intensity of the colors by graying the warm color as much as needed and intensifying the cool color as much as needed. On the far left, the orange would advance and the blue recede in a design. At the far right, the blue would advance and the toned orange would recede.

Contradicting the natural tendencies of color temperature

Although color temperature can be effective in creating dimensionality in some designs, it's not always applicable. Overlapping is another easy, useful way to create a sense of dimensionality. By overlapping one shape over another, you clarify which shape is in front and which is behind. Overlapping helps the eye see placement. It is a particularly important tool in close-up views, such as rooms, detail work, flowers, and glimpses of nature. Examples of overlapping include *Blue Ginkgoes* and *Dreaming of a Room of My Own* (pages 48 and 53). There are numerous examples throughout the book of overlapping, including *The Calm after the Storm, Five Apples, Water Curtain with Orchid, Autumn Walk, Moonlight Sonata, Weeping Willow over Water, Autumn Beauty,* and *Dream of Infinity* (pages 6, 7, 11, 49, 83, 85, and 103).

DREAMING OF A ROOM OF MY OWN by Joen Wolfrom, Fox Island, Washington, 80″ × 94″, 1991

The scene across the water is created through atmospheric perspective. The hills and mountain range in the background become lighter, grayer, and less distinct as they recede into the distance. Because the hill and mountain fabrics are similar in value and tonality, these land elements appear close to each other. The luster on the water is created through subtle value change. This artwork was machine pieced and hand appliquéd.

The most powerful means of creating depth is through *atmospheric perspective.* This is an amazing tool that should be utilized whenever possible, with two exceptions: night scenes and close-ups. If you incorporate atmospheric perspective in designs that have the ability to be dimensional, it will add incredible richness to your art.

The next time you are outside and able to look far into the distance, notice how objects become *grayer* in their coloring, *lighter* in value, *less distinct* in their details, and *smaller* in size as they recede into the distance. If you live in a flat region and are unable to observe this, look at photographic images of landscapes in magazines, books, and calendars. Notice how objects appear grayer, lighter, less distinct, and smaller as they recede into the distance.

In the foreground, the design is usually the most pronounced and detailed, the colors the most intense, and the objects the largest. Each receding layer becomes grayer, lighter, and less distinct. Depending on the design, objects may appear smaller as they recede into the distance.

If you want layers to appear close to each other, make subtle changes in color, value, detail, and size. If you want layers to show a great distance between them, considerably increase the changes in color, value, detail, and size. The background hues will be the grayest (most toned and least intense), the lightest in value, and the least detailed. The illusion of depth can be made subtle or pronounced. Designs that show dimensionality through atmospheric perspective are *Memories of Monet* (right), *Monterey at Dusk, Springtime in the Valley, Dreaming of a Room of My Own,* and *Interwoven* (pages 24, 44, 53, and 116).

Atmospheric perspective can be used in all design styles, although we see it most predominantly in representational designs. With geometric designs, determine the number of layers in your design; then determine the amount of change in value and color for each layer. In *Fantasia* (page 45), two layers were created. *Memories of Monet* uses three layers. Adding dimensionality to your designs will enhance them immeasurably.

Photo by Ken Wagner, Seattle, Washington

MEMORIES OF MONET by Joen Wolfrom, Fox Island, Washington, 70″ × 70″, 2008

This blended-block-design quilt uses atmospheric perspective to create its three-layer design. The large four-pointed stars use the strongest coloring, values, and textures. The softly colored diagonal lattices and background are made with grayer, lighter, and less distinct fabrics than those used in the foreground. (Pattern is available.)

NOTE

If you seek a more in-depth study of color, refer to the book *Color Play.* Besides basic color and color plan information, you will find information on how to create the color illusions of depth, luminosity, luster, transparency, shadows, and highlights. If you want to have a simple color guide when working on your designs, consider using the Ultimate 3-in-1 Color Tool. (Both book and tool are by the author and published by C&T Publishing.)

ACTIVITIES AND EXERCISES

1. To play with color plans, select one color family (page 44). Next, draw a design that you would like to use each day for a week. Using the same design and your selected color family, create the design in a different color plan for the first five days: monochromatic, analogous, complementary, split-complementary, and triadic. After all of the designs are complete, place them on your design wall. Which color combination pleases you most?

Select another color family. Create a new design to use with this color. During each of the next five days, use a different color plan for your design. Repeat this exercise for the next three weeks by selecting a new color family, creating a new design, and remaking the design using that color's five color plans. After all five design sets are complete, view the designs from a distance in random order. Select your favorite three designs. Which of these do you like best? Now regroup the designs by color family. Is there one particular color family that most appeals to you? Next, regroup the images by color plan. Stand back and observe the designs in each plan. Which plan do you like best? Do you find yourself favoring one color family or one color plan over all of the others? What color plan, if any, was difficult for you to use? Which were easy? Take notes of your findings.

2. To play with color temperature, draw a design. Use intense warm colors in the featured objects in the foreground and intense cool colors in the background. Repeat this design, but use toned (grayed) warm hues in the featured foreground objects and toned cool hues in the background. Place these two designs on a design wall and step back. What do you notice?

With the same design, use cool hues for the featured objects in the foreground and warm hues for the background. In order for the foreground objects to advance, they must be more intense than the warm background colors. If the background hues appear too strong, increase the grayness of the warm colors. You want to dilute the warm color's advancing qualities by lessening its intensity. This can be done by shading, tinting, or toning, but it is easiest done through toning. From a distance, look at your design to see if the foreground objects with cool hues appear in front of the warm-colored background. If not, adjust the intensity of both: increase the brightness of the cool hue and make the warm color less bright (for example, make it grayer).

3. To play with color scale, create a design. Make seven additional copies. Each day work on one design:

- Color the design using only pure colors (pure color scale).
- Color the design using only tints (tint scale).
- Color the design using only shades (shade scale).
- Color the design using only tones (tone scale).
- Color the design using the pure color scale as the dominant scale, but use one or more additional scales too.
- Color the design using the tint scale as the dominant scale, but use one or more additional scales too.
- Color the design using the shade scale as the dominant scale, but use one or more additional scales too.
- Color the design using the tone scale as the dominant scale, but use one or more additional scales too.

Place all your designs on the design wall. Which ones do you like most? Which ones appeal to you least? Write down your findings. This should give you a clue as to which scale you prefer and how you like working with that scale.

CHAPTER FIVE

VALUE
Design's Priceless Ingredient

One of the most amazing ingredients in a design is *value*—the lightness or darkness of a color. How you use value in your design is one of the most important choices you can make. Value is an exciting design component. Be sure to take advantage of its superb versatility. It shouldn't be a secret that value plays a more important role than color, but it is. More often than not, color gets the credit, but value does the real work. If you want to create really successful designs, explore the different ways you can play with value.

Using Value to Its Best Advantage

WORKING IN LOW VALUE

Dark shapes are visually heavy. With gravity's pull, these shapes feel most comfortable in the bottom region of a design. Perhaps coincidentally, dark, heavy colors are considered *low in value* or *low value*. *Intertwined* is an example of low-value hues being placed in a design's bottom region. Others include *Lakeside* and *Poulnabrone Dolmen* (pages 63 and 91).

When a design uses mostly low-value colors throughout its surface, it is considered *low key*. In low-key work, it is difficult to see the design without some value contrast. If you prefer to work with dark hues, include one or more lighter values so your design can be seen from a distance.

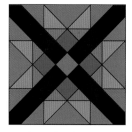

Low-key value;
not enough contrast

Low-key value; lighter
values added for contrast

An example of a low-key design with value contrast is *Northern Lights* (page 110). *Moon Dance* and *Silent Mountain* are two other low-key designs (pages 113 and 120). The value contrast is very important in order to see these designs.

Five Apples (page 7), a low-key design with rich dark colors, is enhanced beautifully with the addition of high-value hues. *Big Bang + 1 Second* (page 94) uses dabs of high-value hues in the midst of very dark, low-value colors. The strength of each design emerges from where the value contrast is most pronounced.

Photo by the artist

INTERTWINED by Carol Taylor, Pittsford, New York, 63″ × 68″, 2004

Carol used value as her featured element to create *Intertwined*. The value change causes our eyes to move from the upper light corner diagonally across the quilt to the darkest hues at the lower corner. The vertical and horizontal lines in each block create repetition, rhythm, and harmony, resulting in great unity.

WORKING IN HIGH VALUE

Light, soft, delicate colors are considered *high in value* or *high value*. These hues appear to float upward toward the sky in visual weightlessness. Most often, we expect high-value colors to be in the upper regions of a design. A design made primarily from high-value colors is considered *high key*. If a design uses only closely related high-value hues, the design will appear washed out or faded. If you are working in high key, make certain you have some value contrast within that key's range.

Contrast in close-value designs adds interest and helps viewers' eyes find the focus. In *Social Climber Roses*, notice the beautifully subtle value changes in the roses, moving from very light to medium values. If the rose petals had used only a few steps of value change, the blossoms would not be as gorgeous. *Baskets & Blossoms*, a high-key design, is enhanced by its value contrast. Another example of high-key value use is *5 of Clubs* (page 89).

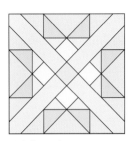

High-key value;
not enough contrast

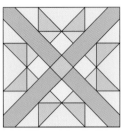

High-key value; darker
values added for contrast

Photo by Ken Wagner, Seattle, Washington

BASKETS & BLOSSOMS by Alex Anderson, Livermore, California,
50″ × 50″, 2006

The soft delicacy of this blended-block-design quilt is due to the light values used in its coloring. With few exceptions, the colors are high value. Therefore, this quilt is considered a high-key design. (Pattern is available.)

Photo by the artist

SOCIAL CLIMBER ROSES by Melinda Bula, El Dorado Hills, California,
34″ × 48″, 2005

Social Climber Roses illustrates exquisite use of value. Melinda moves the rose values from blush pink to a dark reddish hue, using scores of fabrics. Her value steps are so perfect that these roses appear lifelike. The low-value (dark green) background allows the roses to be the highlight of this design. *Social Climber Roses* was exhibited at the Shelburne Museum in Vermont in 2008.

PLAYING THE MIDDLE

Colors that are neither dark nor light are considered *middle value.* If a design uses mostly middle-value hues, it is a *middle-key* design. It is very important to include value contrast in middle-key designs. If only middle-value hues are used, designs can disappear or appear flat. Adding some value contrast makes a difference in the success of middle-key designs.

Middle-key value;
not enough contrast

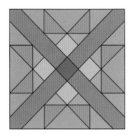

Middle-key value; lighter or
darker values added for contrast

Middle-key designs with good value contrast are *House through Arch, Mountain Chapel, The Wedding Quilt,* and *The Girls of Tyrone Farm* (pages 9, 28, 34, and 88).

Value is an important tool when creating. You can use it in your design in unlimited ways. Determining what part of the design will be the lightest and darkest can make interesting differences in your design. Notice how the same colors and values can be used differently in the same design. Play with value to see how it best suits your design.

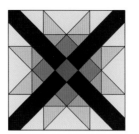 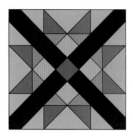

Values used differently in each block

Two designs that use value beautifully are *Amazon Star* and *Thistle Pods* by Judy and Brad Niemeyer. In *Thistle Pods,* there is strong, defined value contrast, which accentuates this vibrant design. In *Amazon Star,* both high and low value contrasts are present, but there are more value steps between the two extremes. This value use creates quite a different effect, as the colors vibrate with the combination of close values and strong contrast. In *Sedona,* the values are defined in clear steps of lights, mediums, and darks. The combination of value and color use brings about a rich, strong design. These three designs illustrate different ways to use value. The sky is the limit with value play.

AMAZON STAR by Judy and Brad Niemeyer, Kalispell, Montana, 104″ × 104″, 2008

This fabulous circular-design quilt offers a full value range of hues to stunning effect. These hues are mostly toned, so they exude a quiet richness, which is perfect for most homes. The reiteration of star-point shapes throughout the design creates wonderful unity. This foundation paper-pieced quilt has a contemporary feel with its use of Bali batiks. (Pattern is available.)

THISTLE PODS by Judy and Brad Niemeyer, Kalispell, Montana, 96″ × 96″, 2007

The strong value contrast in *Thistle Pods* creates a dynamic design. The dark Bali batik fabrics are dramatically paired with delicate background hues. This dark/light value contrast further accentuates the beauty of the thistle pods' and star points' slender shapes. (Foundation-piecing pattern is available.)

SEDONA by Sally Collins, Walnut Creek, California, 45½″ × 45½″, 2001

Inspired by the traditional block Carpenter's Wheel, Sally created a gorgeous original design that uses value to great advantage. Streaks of blush coral and a deep, rich brown are the two value extremes. Between these two values, Sally has used several different value steps to bring strength and clarity to her design. The colors give this a Southwestern flair; value provides the beautiful visual flow.

THE VALUE OF COLOR IS RELATIVE

The value of a color is relative. A color can appear light or dark or seem to disappear altogether—all in one design.

In the first column of the illustration below, middle-value green, violet, and orange look quite dark next to the light-value tints. In the middle column, the same three colors are next to similarly valued hues. They blend into the group. In the right column, the three middle-value colors look quite light next to the dark-value hues. In fact, they appear visually lighter than they do in the left column, yet they are all exactly the same value in all three examples. This illustration helps to show how the same color can disappear or appear too light or too dark within a design, depending on the value of the surrounding hues.

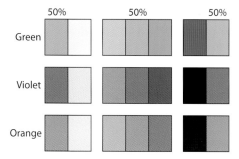

A color can look light or dark depending on what color or value it is next to.

Each value scale (on the right) moves from light to dark. A middle-value color from each scale is placed in a vertical strip down the center of its scale. The same color appears dark with the light hues, light with the dark hues, and seemingly disappears in the middle-value area. Yet, this thin strip is the exact same color from top to bottom. This illustration shows clearly how dramatically a color can appear to change, due simply to the value of its neighboring hues.

Color is relative. Notice how dark and light each vertical strip looks as it moves from the top to the bottom of its value range—yet each strip is exactly the same color from top to bottom.

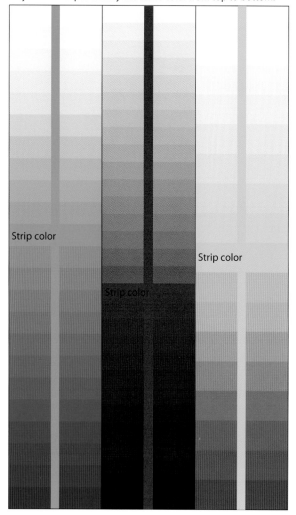

Value scale

If a shape looks too dark in its setting, the surrounding hues are too light. Conversely, if a shape looks too light, the surrounding colors are too dark. If a shape disappears in a design, its value is too similar to the values of its neighboring colors. If you understand that the lightness or darkness of a color is affected by the values of its neighbors, you will have more control over your designs. You can resolve design problems that arise from value placement. This understanding will enable you to work very creatively with value.

Using Value Creatively

We expect to see the darkest values at the bottom of a design, as seen in *Lakeside* (page 63). The dramatic scene in *Poulnabrone Dolmen* (page 91) also uses value in the position we naturally expect. However, switching the expected value position can be quite stunning. *Tidal Flat* (page 104) provides strong drama in its atypical placement of high-value hues in the bottom section of this image. Dare to be evocative in your use of value if it works in your design.

There are endless ways to move value through a design's surface. *I've Been to Mecca* (page 7) uses subtle gradation to create beauty and interest. *The Colour of Jazz, It's About Time* (this page), and *Inner City / Outer Space* (page 62) show very innovative value use. Look through both Gallery 1 (pages 6–11) and Gallery 2 (pages 83–95) to see other artworks that use value in an interesting way.

IT'S ABOUT TIME by Janet Steadman, Whidbey Island, Washington, 52″ × 67″, 2002

It's About Time uses value as its featured element. The lightest values lead the eye from the design's top edge to its suggestive apex in the lower region. The contrast in value creates wonderful intrigue and drama. *It's About Time* was awarded the Best of Show at the 2004 Association of Pacific Northwest Quilters exhibition.

Photo by Roger Schreiber, Seattle, Washington

THE COLOUR OF JAZZ by Stacie Littlejohn, Wallacetown, Ontario, Canada, 60″ × 76″, 2009

Stacie's two-color quilt beautifully illustrates value as the featured design element. Moving values from light to dark in opposing directions in the background and the foreground creates dimensionality and spaciousness. Each motif is made from its own fabric, so there are wonderful subtle differences in both intensity and tonality in this quilt. The border is well integrated with the design, as it uses the same colors and motifs as the central design. This quilt was made from the Starburst Mosaic pattern designed by Camille Remme (Me PUBNS).

INNER CITY / OUTER SPACE by Robin M. Haller, Carbondale, Illinois, 95″ × 85″, 1998

Robin selected value as the featured element in *Inner City / Outer Space*. Working in a geometric style, she created a beautifully intricate tessellated design that offers repetition, unity, and variety.

Photo by the artist

In *Interwoven* (page 116), Linda Beach featured strong value contrast amid subtle middle-value hues. Beth Miller chose to focus primarily on middle-value hues in *Dandelions and Rust*, but she incorporated both high and low values for contrast and interest. Without these contrasting values, the design would disappear before our eyes.

DANDELIONS AND RUST by Beth Miller, Kambah, Australian Capital Territory, Australia, 25″ × 35″, 2009

This subtle design is an amazingly complex study of value in a limited color palette. With value being the featured element, Beth's challenge was to create a design using only a rusted curtain material with hues that ranged from soft cream to deep brown. The subtle design is created with value moving from high to low. Notice how much detail is created with this limited color palette.

Photo by David Paterson, Canberra, Australian Capital Territory, Australia

Moving value through your design is a great strategy: It creates interest, moves the eye, and can be quite dramatic. As color changes from light to dark, it appears as if light is hitting the lightest areas but not the darker ones. If you like the idea of incorporating luster into your artwork, use subtle value steps to create the effect. In *Lakeside* (page 63), the close value gradation in the sky and water creates luster. The soft, close value steps in *Social Climber Roses* (page 57) create luster on the rose petals. Notice the luster in *Ma, How Come She Gets All the Attention?* and *Unnamed Log Cabin* (pages 103 and 126).

LAKESIDE by Gloria Loughman, Drysdale, Victoria, Australia, 25″ × 20″, 2010

Lakeside beautifully illustrates the full range of value in a design. The darkest hues are at the bottom, giving the landscape strength. Small portions of these dark hues are reiterated in the tree, which carries the visual weight upward. The gentle value change in sky and water create a beautiful lustrous effect.

Photo by Anthony Loughman, Drysdale, Victoria, Australia

A DREAM OF SWIMMING POINTS by Marian Henstra, Aerdenhout, the Netherlands, 41¼″ × 54″, 2010

In this surreal design, sea creatures appear to be swimming in a circular fashion. Value plays an important role in this design, as the dark and light values coming together create a dramatic effect. This is greatly enhanced by the center area's luminous yellow-green hues. The flowing curved lines of the swimming creatures promote a sense of movement.

Photo by the artist

A Dream of Swimming Points uses value to create luster. Other good examples of designs that use value to create luster include *House through Arch, Dreaming of a Room of My Own, Boxing Out,* and *Kimberley Mystique* (pages 9, 53, 90, and 92).

ACTIVITIES AND EXERCISES

1. Visit art/craft galleries, museums, and exhibitions. Determine the value key (pages 56–58) you are most drawn to and the one you like least. Write down your findings for future reference.

2. Select the ten artworks you are most drawn to in this book. Determine each one's value key and use of value. Then select the ten artworks that you like least. What is the value key of each and how is value used? Write down your findings. Analyze your likes and dislikes with regard to value use.

3. Look at your designs from the past year or two. How have you worked with value? What value key did you work in? Do you find value problems? Write down your findings.

4. After spending time observing art in galleries, museums, and this book, analyze your own work. Determine how you would like to use value in your next projects.

5. With paper, fabric and gluestick, paint, colored pencils, chalk, or other materials, create the following value exercises.

a. Create a design that moves the value from light in the central area to dark in the outer perimeter.

b. Create a design that moves the value from dark in the central area to light at the outer perimeter.

c. Create two designs that move the value from one corner area to the diagonally opposite area. In one design, work with the darkest values at the bottom; reverse the values on the second design.

d. Create a lustrous design using close value steps.

e. Create a design that moves value in the background but not the foreground. Then create another design that moves value in the foreground but not the background.

f. Make at least two designs that use value in innovative ways.

CHAPTER SIX

Spicing Up Your Design
with TEXTURE

Texture adds extra spice and visual richness to a design. Designs are easily enhanced by textural changes: combining smoothness, roughness, and patterning. Texture adds beauty to artwork when it is done well; it allows subtle changes in the surface design. A smooth surface can appear sleek and elegant; however, too much smoothness can cause the design to appear flat. A textured surface can be slightly flecked or obscured, or it can be so strongly textured that it appears rough. Texture adds character, can create a sense of age, and provides uniqueness. When the texture creates a pattern, it adds detail, richness, and interest. Each design suggests a different textural application. Assess your design to see how you can apply texture to good advantage.

If you are a painter, texture depends on your tool of choice—brush, knife, sponge, stamp, fingers, palm, and so on. There is an amazing array of items that give unusual texture when used to apply paint. Keep your eyes open to new ways to provide texture in your designs.

As a quiltmaker or fabric artist, you have countless choices for texture—thread, yarn, buttons, fabric, paint, paper, beads, doodads, and many more; be creative. As you look though this book, you'll notice different uses of these materials to create texture.

Many of us have not delved into the textural world to take advantage of what it offers to a work of art. In this chapter, the artwork featured is extraordinary because of its textural effects. Some designs are complicated and challenging. Regardless of the time or expertise needed to create them, they all should provide us with inspiration and a realization that texture can play an extremely important role in design. For some works of art, texture is the obvious featured element. For others, it supports and enhances. There are at least a dozen more artworks in this book that could have been featured in this chapter, so be certain to wander through the pages to find more unbelievable works of art that show breathtakingly beautiful examples of texture.

Extraordinary Textural Effects

Nostalgia is a design that features texture. Ludmila Aristova used appliqué and hand embroidery to create this nostalgic floral design that hints of bygone days. Her bouquet is filled with a wonderful selection of intricate flowers and berries. It is rare to see beautiful hand embroidery in a free-flowing design such as this.

Photo by D. James Dee, New York, New York

NOSTALGIA by Ludmila Aristova,
Brooklyn, New York, 34″ × 26″, 2007

Texture is what captures the eyes first in *Nostalgia*. Ludmila's beautiful hand embroidery and appliqué create a magical glimpse of the flowers found in gardens everywhere. In this asymmetrical design, flowers, petals, leaves, and berries are used to create balance through color and value placement. Notice that some of the seeds and berries move into the border for more flexibility in attaining visual weight.

In *Daydreams* (page 67), Dineke Ugen created amazing texture in her design's background through her varied selection of fabrics. This quilt illustrates extremely well how attention to fabric texture can provide a rich tapestry background. Consider creating a beautifully textured fabric background for your design.

Kay D. Haerland's *Under the Canopy* (page 67) is a stunning display of textural eloquence depicting an Australian rain forest. The textural detail in this artwork is amazing. Each time you look at this artwork, you will surely find some new detail that escaped your notice previously. *Under the Canopy*

is so realistic that it is as if we are standing before the forest waiting to enter.

In Barbara Shapel's *In Hiding* we are unaware of the threadwork as we look at the full view of the scene. We are engrossed in the beauty of the scene. Then as we acclimate ourselves, we realize that the blue heron is a visual surprise that we had not anticipated. His threadwork plays a major textural role in this design. In this detail image, we see the threadwork from the back side. The exquisite detailing makes the heron look real.

Photo by Mark Frey, Yelm, Washington

IN HIDING by Barbara Shapel, Washougal, Washington, 38″ × 75″, 2008

This overall view of *In Hiding* gives you reference when viewing the detail of the elegant blue heron from the back side.

Photo by Mark Frey, Yelm, Washington

In Hiding, detail. Thread painting creates beautiful texture, as can be seen in this detail view of the elegant blue heron from the back side of *In Hiding.* The blue heron looks real with his exquisite feathers. Barbara used rayon thread for her thread painting. Notice the textural effect created by the background quilting.

UNDER THE CANOPY by Kay D. Haerland, Green Point, New South Wales, Australia, 60½″ × 47″, 2010

Under the Canopy gives us a chance to feast our eyes on the beautiful textures and colors of an Australian rain forest in this glorious representation. The detail in Kay's scene is quite amazing with a multitude of textures provided for our visual pleasure. Asymmetrical balance has been attained through the careful placement of shapes, colors, and values.

DAYDREAMS by Dineke Ugen, Roden, the Netherlands, 43¼″ × 24¾″, 2007

Dineke created this striking design using scores of fabrics that are filled with luscious textures and patterns. Her selection of background fabrics creates fantastic visual richness and interest. Nonobjective shapes flow across the background in an interesting curving design, moving our eyes along the design from one side to the other. These shapes, too, are filled with interesting patterns and textures. Asymmetrical balance is created in *Daydreams* through the use of color, value, shapes, and direction.

Repetition creates the beautiful rhythm seen in *Autumn* by Ludmila Aristova. This repetition of flittering shapes and color creates wonderful unity. As you can see, this artwork is filled with glorious texture. In fact, *Autumn* shows the exquisite detailing that reveals the artist's background in fine sewing. Born in Russia, Ludmila graduated from the Moscow Textile Institute and became a designer of one-of-a-kind fashion garments. You can see her expertise in this artwork, as well as in *Nostalgia* and *Summer Rain* (pages 65 and 86).

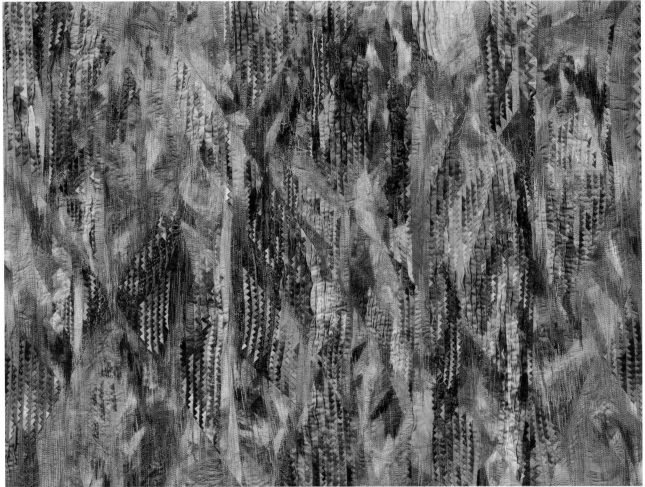

AUTUMN by Ludmila Aristova,
Brooklyn, New York, 46″ × 34″, 2003

The minute textural details in *Autumn* add much richness to this exquisite design. The repetition of flittering shapes and color creates beautiful rhythm and harmony. Unity, contrast, and variation are seen throughout. The masterful creation of texture through fabric manipulation gives us a glimpse into Ludmila's in-depth sewing background. After graduating from the Moscow Textile Institute, she designed one-of-a-kind fashion garments for Moscow art salons and for her own private clients. She creates her one-of-a-kind textile art with equal flair. Ludmila used nonobjective shapes to create this nonobjective work of art.

In *Summer Serves Fall,* Janett Rice placed loosely woven red lamé fabric over leaf shapes. Then the lamé was quilted in small circles with gold metallic thread. Janett double-stitched the small circles; added flat, bright gold pearl beads; and then quilted a circular pattern with variegated gold, orange, and red thread on the background of batik fabric. This small free-flowing artwork is filled with textural interest.

In *Autumn Orchard,* Kathie Briggs brings us beautiful richness through texture in both her trees and the orchard carpet. The design is filled with small surprises of interest. Kathie used hand-dyed and commercial cotton, hand-dyed cheesecloth, and beads to create the textural effects in her design.

Photo by the artist

AUTUMN ORCHARD by Kathie Briggs, Charlevoix, Michigan, 33″ × 11½″, 2005

Autumn Orchard beautifully illustrates the use of texture as a featured element. Kathie used hand-dyed and commercial cotton, hand-dyed cheesecloth, and beads to create the textural effects in her design. The detailed texture in the artwork is intricate and beautifully done. The repetition of trees in an extended horizontal format creates an overall horizontal effect.

Photo by the artist

SUMMER SERVES FALL by Janett Rice, Henderson, Nevada, 16″ × 21″, 2009

To create texture, Janett put loosely woven red lamé fabric over leaf shapes; quilted the lamé in small circles with gold metallic thread; double-stitched the small circles; added flat, bright gold pearl beads; and then quilted a circular pattern with variegated gold, orange, and red thread on the background's autumnal batik fabric. The softly curving design, filled with interest, moves our eyes across the artwork.

Rosa Celeste, detail 1

Rosa Celeste, detail 2

Rosa Celeste, detail 3

Texture should be unique to each design. Although most designs use texture to enhance, some designs use texture as their theme. The gorgeous design of the wholecloth quilt *Rosa Celeste* is created with threadwork. This amazing work of thread art by Annette Valtl was extremely difficult to execute because of its intricacy and its size. In this artwork, texture is everything—it creates the line, direction, color, texture, and movement.

Photos by the artist

ROSA CELESTE by Annette Valtl, Remscheid, Germany, 77″ × 77″, 2009

Annette's *Rosa Celeste* was inspired by the work of Hartmut Warm, a civil engineer by training but an independent researcher in astronomy and geometry. His book *Signature of the Celestial Spheres* discusses his discoveries relating to the solar system and its inherent order. His fascinating work and amazing graphs were the design basis of *Rosa Celeste*, a stunning wholecloth quilt.

Although Annette found the intricate drafting and stitching challenging because of the necessary exactness, the size of the quilt, and the cloth's pliability, it was well worth the effort. *Rosa Celeste* illustrates how stitching lines can be exquisite when thoughtful planning and great designs are combined. Annette used hand-dyed silk and cotton fabrics, wool batting, and polyester thread.

Kimberley Mystique, detail (full quilt on page 92)

Pat Durbin's beautiful threadwork provides wonderful lifelike texture in *Winter Walk* (page 16). Besides her threadwork, Pat's fabric choices for the tree bark are superb. Paula Nadelstern's *Cheddar Cheese* (page 21) kaleidoscope is exquisite in its use of fabric to create texture. She used cottons and hand-marbled silk by Cosette Russell. Gloria Loughman has created stunning textures in *Kimberley Mystique* (above and page 92). The detailed intricacy is glorious. Barbara Ortez's *Silent Mountain* (page 120) is not only beautiful because of her use of value, but the textural choices of each fabric add richness to her design. Notice how no fabric accidentally distracts our eyes. She has carefully selected fabrics that have the same tonality, so they work as a textural unit.

As you thumb through this book's pages, you'll find scores of wonderful textural effects in other artwork. Study the different ways the artists created their textures. Keep your eyes open for intriguing examples of texture. Keep your camera handy to take your own textural images for inspiration. To whet your textural appetite, enjoy the sampling of textures on page 72.

LESS IS MORE

The artwork in this chapter features texture. However, texture is not always the featured element of a design. It is your decision when and how it will be featured. When you decide to make it the featured element, don't be overindulgent in its use. Too much texture can lead to busyness. Also, an overabundance of texture can cause the viewer's eyes to be overwhelmed and not know where to look. Assess your design and determine where texture is needed and which types of texture should be included. It is not necessary to cover every inch of your design with attention-getting texture. Consider quiet space. Use a variety of textures in differing strengths. Don't have all the textures be the same visual strength. Enjoy playing with texture.

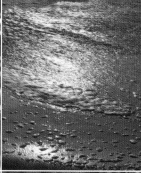

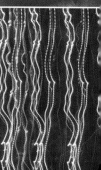

ACTIVITIES AND EXERCISES

1. Look at your past designs. How did you use texture in your designs? Would you like to change your use of texture? What would you like to do? How will you begin?

2. Begin a file for your texture collection. In this file, place photos or samples of wonderful textural examples for future reference. These can be photos or images from magazines, calendars, the Internet, or other resources. Before beginning your next project, think about how you would like to incorporate texture into the design.

3. Play with paint and textures even if you are not a painter by nature. Use at least twelve different objects from your home or studio to apply paint to the selected design surface—no brushes. Use your imagination. See how innovative you can be. At another time, gather all your painting brushes and experiment with the different textures each offers.

4. Create one design each day for a month. Try to create designs that will feature texture or in which texture will be highly supportive and visible in the design. Be imaginative in your textural use. Work with both man-made products and nature. Try to expand your textural use each day.

If you are a fabric artist, be open to using all types of fabrics, since each has its own textural effect. For instance, silk is luscious and smooth, yet raw silk is nubby; burlap is rough; velvet is rich and thick; and cotton is smooth and flat. Use the fabric that provides the texture you wish to achieve.

5. If you are interested in expanding your use of creative texture, study the fascinating photography montages in the small book *Dreamscapes: Exploring Photo Montages* by André Gallant. This book provides amazing examples of texture in photography that are unlike any you will have seen previously.

6. In your next design project, determine how you will use texture to add beauty and interest. Work in a manner that you have not tried previously in your designs.

Additional Suggestions for Specific Designers

QUILTERS   If you are a quilter, make five copies of your proposed quilt top (approximate size = 8″ × 11″). With a pencil, a ruler, and any other tools you'd like to use, draw lines to accentuate the beauty of your design with quilting. Try to draw five different quilting-design variations. Choose one of these designs as your quilting design. If you use a professional quilter, take all five designs to her. Show her your favorite. Then discuss the design and any adaptations she may need to make for technical reasons.

PROFESSIONAL QUILTERS   When you are given a project to quilt, look at the design as a whole. Try to come up with three quilting-design possibilities. Use the one that you think best suits the overall design. Don't let your expertise and exuberance in the quilting stitch lead to the textural element becoming more important than intended. Use your talent and skill to enhance the design.

CHAPTER SEVEN

VISUAL FINESSE
Proportion *and* Scale

When proportion and scale are used well in design, we rarely think of these elements. It's almost as if they don't exist. However, if proportion and scale are not dealt with well in a design, they visually cry for attention. They can make an enormous difference—the difference between a poor, a mediocre, and a fantastic design is amazing. Be aware of their quiet importance as you develop your art. As a silent partner, they ask for so little, yet they bring so much to your design.

Proportion

Proportion relates to how shapes interact with each other within a design. Shapes that are proportionate to each other look good together. It's your choice as to the size of shapes your design needs. The sizes of the shapes in *Five Apples* and *Arabian Nights* are quite different from each other, but within each design the shapes work well together because they are proportionate (pages 7 and 77). This also holds true for *Overrun*.

If the shapes in your design are in good proportion to each other, your design should come together easily. If you find that one of your shapes is much larger than the others, it is a more challenging task to make the design work. When a shape takes on too much *unintentional* notoriety because its size is out of proportion, it can be visually distracting or jarring. For instance, the vase below is much too large for its flowers. The vase's size overwhelms the flowers and diminishes their importance because the shapes are out of proportion.

OVERRUN by Charlotte Warr Andersen, Salt Lake City, Utah, 70" × 26", 2004

In this gathering, the rabbits are in proportion to one another. The largest rabbit catches our eye because it appears slightly larger and his coloring is a bit different, but these differences are not enough to stop our eyes from moving through the line of rabbits. Charlotte used a 4:1 ratio (pages 77–81) for her central design, which allowed her to spread the rabbits out in a comfortable setting. The ratio changed slightly when the borders were added.

FIGURE 7-1
This vase is too large for the flowers.

Fortunately, a proportional problem can be resolved easily. The large vase can be replaced by one that is smaller and in proportion to the flowers.

FIGURE 7-2
The sizes of the flower bouquet and vase relate well to each other. Because they are proportional, they make a beautiful statement together.

There may be times when you want to exaggerate a shape or use disproportionate shapes. If so, have some visual continuity between these shapes. To be successful, the shape should be an integral part of the design. In *Enchanted Journey,* the featured butterfly has been exaggerated in size, so our eyes go right to it. The addition of many other butterflies of varying sizes helps to create visual continuity in the design. Also, the large butterfly's size disparity is minimized by a range in sizes among the other shapes.

ENCHANTED JOURNEY by Kay D. Haerland, Green Point, New South Wales, Australia, 73½″ × 54″, 1998

In *Enchanted Journey,* Kay features a butterfly that is exaggerated in size. To guide our eyes through the design, she has provided a plentitude of smaller butterflies to act as a visual gradation bridge, moving our eyes through the scene with the aid of butterflies, large to small.

Photo by Bard Haerland

In Robin Haller's *Leaving Ireland,* the large colorful stones are integrated into the design by a plentiful gradation of stones of varying sizes. In addition, Robin has reiterated the stone's colors in the sky, albeit in softer hues. This helps partner the sky with the stones. The darkest blues in the water at the bottom right also help distribute the visual weight throughout the bottom section of the scene.

LEAVING IRELAND by Robin M. Haller, Carbondale, Illinois, 70″ × 86″, 2006

The large stones in this intriguing design first attract our attention because of their size. Robin has integrated these stones into the design by including many other stones of varying sizes in the scene. The carefully placed deep blue water also helps distribute the visual weight. The subtly colored sky is pieced in the Double Irish Chain design.

Photo by the artist

PLAYING WITH PROPORTION IN NUMBER SEQUENCES

If you love designs that appear to have a visual rhythm in their shapes' sizes, you might enjoy using number sequences. The most renowned proportional number sequence is the *Fibonacci sequence.* Although this number sequence was well recognized centuries earlier in Greece and India, Leonardo Fibonacci brought it to the attention of European mathematicians in the twelfth century. The Fibonacci sequence highlights the strong relationship between mathematics, nature, and art. Nature uses this numerical sequence in amazing fashion, as you can see in nautilus shells, pinecones, flower petals, flower heads, and the growth patterns and growth rates of plants, animals, and humans. Besides mathematics and nature, the Fibonacci sequence is used in art and architecture.

The Fibonacci sequence begins as 0, 1, 1, 2, 3, 5, 8, 13, 21, 34, 55, 89, 144, and so on. Each successive number in this sequence is the sum of the previous two numbers. You can use small or large sections of this sequence to determine the dimensions of elements within a design. Caryl Bryer Fallert's *Fibonacci's Garden* is a beautiful example of a design using the Fibonacci sequence. The latticework in this artwork is pieced from two fabrics that were cut into strips and pieced in an orderly progression using the Fibonacci sequence. Additionally, the series of circles are gradated in both size and color in two arcs across the surface of the lattice. Notice the fluidity of the design created by the use of this arithmetic sequence.

Photo by the artist

FIBONACCI'S GARDEN by Caryl Bryer Fallert, Paducah, Kentucky, 54″ × 71″, 1995

Caryl used the Fibonacci sequence to create her fascinating *Fibonacci's Garden*. The circular pathway leads our eyes upward through the design. As you study this design, you will notice that more than one set of number sequences is included. This design is placed in a 3:4 ratio (pages 77–81).

FINAL THOUGHTS ABOUT PROPORTION

Unless you are doing something unusual, your shapes and objects should be in good proportion to each other. To make certain your design has good proportion, stand back several feet to see if the shapes are working well together. If any shape stands out too much because of its size, make the necessary changes. If you are using an out-of-proportion shape on purpose, make certain it is well integrated in the design.

Scale

Scale refers to a composition and its total design surface—its size and its configuration. It relates to how the components within a design fit into the space provided. There should be a sense of comfort between the components in a design and the space that holds them—the total design surface.

Your use of scale can make the difference between a beautiful design and a visually uncomfortable one. If a design appears too tight in its boundaries or it seems overwhelmed by the space that holds it, the scale is incorrect. The small vase of flowers on the large table looks dwarfed and insignificant, illustrating poor scale.

FIGURE 7-3
The small vase on the large table illustrates poor use of scale. The table better accommodates a larger vase of flowers that feels comfortable in the space.

FIGURE 7-4
This bouquet of flowers looks beautiful here because the table vsually accomodates it. The size of the table—its overall scale—is right for this bouquet.

SELECTING YOUR DESIGN'S RATIO

One powerful way to help your design evolve to its highest potential is to select the width and height dimensions that promote the natural movement of your design. It's important not to just wing it. In other words, don't just choose any random width to go with a selected height; nor should you choose a random height to go with a particular width. Instead, select your dimensions based on a ratio that best suits your design. Observing your design's directional flow and focus gives you a starting point to sort through your options. Once you understand how your design is evolving, look through the different ratios to see which one would work best for your composition. When you determine the specific ratio, you probably will need to make some changes so that your composition and surface dimensions work as partners.

We witness incorrect use of scale daily: A small cabin is visually overwhelmed on an expansive site, while an enormous house placed on a tiny piece of property is overwhelming, as is large furniture that dwarfs a room. A large tree in a small garden and a dwarf tree in a huge garden both represent incorrect use of scale.

Poor scale choice may be due to not knowing how to determine dimensions that provide a comfortable and workable space for a composition. For this reason, I have included the following information about ratios and dimensions, which have so much to do with scale.

ARABIAN NIGHTS by Ricky Tims, LaVeta, Colorado, 51″ × 51″, 2009

This beautiful radiating medallion design is best placed in a square—a 1:1 ratio. The shapes vary in size, but they are in good proportion to each other. Because the scale and proportion work well, these two elements are not a concern in this quilt. (Pattern is available.)

Photo by Ken Wagner, Seattle, Washington

1:1 Ratio

A *1:1 ratio* is a perfect ratio for designs that radiate symmetrically from a center point (see Figure 7-6, page 79). For example, if your design is 24″ high in this ratio, it will also be 24″ wide. *Arabian Nights* is an excellent example of this ratio.

Eye-Catching Eyespot (page 80) is a perfect design for a 1:1 ratio. If the butterfly had been alone in the design without the lines, the butterfly might appear overwhelmed in its space. However, with the lines moving our eyes from the butterfly onward, there is a sense of visual comfort and intrigue. This is an excellent example of *less is more,* as the design is profound in its clarity.

A 1:1 ratio is not a good option for a design that has good vertical or horizontal movement, because this ratio doesn't provide enough room for this type of directional movement. Also, a 1:1 ratio is a very difficult ratio to use for asymmetrical designs. If you choose a 1:1 ratio for an asymmetrical design, you will need to place your design's major focus off-center to create good visual balance. Successful asymmetrical designs in a 1:1 ratio are *Georgette Tulips* and *Oak Veiling* (pages 32 and 113).

Photo by Ken Wagner, Seattle, Washington

TICONDEROGA STAR by Larisa Key, Willimantic, Connecticut; quilted by Gail B. Federowicz; 78″ × 98″, 2008

Set in a 3:4 ratio, *Ticonderoga Star* looks as if it may be an on-point design, although it is not. Larisa designed three Four Patch blocks to make a well-integrated blended-block design. Notice how effectively the border works to keep our eyes engaged with the central design. (Pattern is available.)

1:2, 1:3, 1:4—Three Ratios for Elongated Designs

A *1:2 ratio* provides added width to a horizontal design or it extends height to a vertical design. In this ratio, the longer dimension is twice as long as the shorter one (see Figure 7-9, page 79). If you want one dimension to be 24″ wide, the other dimension would be double that—48″ high. If you want the long dimension of your design to be 60″, the other dimension would be 30″. *Poulnabrone Dolmen* (page 91) features a 1:2 ratio.

If your design needs more lengthwise extension than a 1:2 ratio provides, consider a *1:3 ratio.* In this ratio, one dimension is three times greater than the other dimension (see Figure 7-10, page 79). This gives more room for the design to expand in one direction. Thus, if you want one dimension of your design to be 24″, the other dimension would be 72″. The dimensions of *Acid Rain* (page 80) are in a 1:3 ratio. As you can see, this ratio allows for a dynamic sky to evolve.

A *1:4 ratio* greatly exaggerates the length of a design. One dimension is four times greater than the other dimension (see Figure 7-11, page 79). If you want your 24″-high design to have an extreme horizontal extension, the 1:4 ratio would give you a width of 96″. *Rhododendrons over Water* (page 33) is in a 1:4 ratio. The design surface (without the border framing) of *Overrun* (page 74) is also in a 1:4 ratio.

3:4 Ratio

The *3:4 ratio* is best used when a design has only slightly more movement in one direction than the other (see Figure 7-6, page 79). In a 3:4 ratio, a design that is 24″ in one direction would be 32″ in the other direction. If you want your design to be 60″ in the longest dimension, the shorter dimension would be 45″. The 3:4 ratio should be saved for such occasions when your design does not need much expansion in one direction or the other. Examples of artworks that fit well in a 3:4 ratio are *Ticonderoga Star* and *Galaxy* (left and page 99).

2:3 Ratio

Although many people use the 3:4 ratio for their designs, most designs are better suited to a ratio that provides more directional movement. You will be surprised at how effectively a ratio change can enhance the beauty of your design. A *2:3 ratio* allows for more extended directional movement than a 3:4 ratio does (Figure 7-7, page 79). It doesn't exaggerate the length as much as the 1:2, 1:3, and 1:4 ratios do. It provides a comfortable space within which to work. See *5 of Clubs* and *Fishermen's Widows* (pages 89 and 114) for examples of a 2:3 ratio.

SELECT YOUR DESIGN'S DIMENSIONS FROM THE FOLLOWING RATIOS

24″

24″

1:1 ratio

1 × 1 = 1
1 × 24 = 24
24″ × 24″

FIGURE 7-5

32″

24″

3:4 ratio

24 ÷ 3 = 8
4 × 8 = 32
24″ × 32″

FIGURE 7-6

36″

24″

2:3 ratio

24 ÷ 2 = 12
12 × 3 = 36
24″ × 36″

FIGURE 7-7

39″

24″

8:13 ratio

24 ÷ 8 = 3
3 × 13 = 39
24″ × 39″

FIGURE 7-8

48″

24″

1:2 ratio

24 × 2 = 48
24″ × 48″

FIGURE 7-9

72″

24″

1:3 ratio

24 × 3 = 72
24″ × 72″

FIGURE 7-10

96″

24″

1:4 ratio

24 × 4 = 96
24″ × 96″

FIGURE 7-11

ACID RAIN by Gloria Loughman, Drysdale, Victoria, Australia, 20″ × 60″, 2009

In this stunning landscape, Gloria placed her trees in a narrow rectangular format using a 1:3 ratio. This gave her the space to accentuate the dying trees and to create a dramatic sky. The textures used in the fabrics enhance the haunting beauty of this artwork.

EYE-CATCHING EYESPOT
by Inge Mardal and Steen Hougs, Chantilly, France, 47¼″ × 47¼″, 2003

Eye-Catching Eyespot illustrates well that a clean, clear design can be eye-catching and dramatic. Our eyes go directly to the single butterfly. Once there, our attention is attracted to the fine lines that move toward the corners. Notice that the lines do not go to the corner where our eyes can become trapped. Instead they are placed where our eyes can easily move back to the butterfly. These lines provide visual interaction and make it possible for the butterfly to be visually comfortable in this scale. Using a 1:1 ratio and a rule-of-thirds focus structure (Chapter 9, pages 108–121), this solitary butterfly is well placed in its setting.

NOTE

If you need to convert inches into centimeters, multiply the number of inches by 2.54. For example, 12″ × 2.54 = 30.48 centimeters. To convert centimeters into inches, divide the number of centimeters by 2.54. For example, 90 centimeters divided by 2.54 = 35.43″ (approximately 35½″).

8:13 Ratio— The Golden Mean

It is believed that the most beautiful, pleasing dimension for art and architecture is based on the ratio of the *golden mean* (or *golden section*), 8:13. It provides beautifully balanced dimensions (Figure 7-8 page 79). Interestingly, the golden mean ratio is a component of the Fibonacci sequence (page 76).

If your design has good directional movement and one direction's movement does not need to be exaggerated, seriously consider using the golden mean ratio for your design's dimensions. More than likely, this subtle dimensional change will enhance your design beautifully. This ratio should not be used when your design needs to exaggerate one length or when you have a design that radiates symmetrically from a center point. *Five Apples* (page 7) is a beautiful example of dimensions using an 8:13 ratio.

The exact golden mean ratio is 1:1.618 or 8:12.944. The latter can be rounded to 8:13, which results in a 1:1.625 ratio. This ratio is used to determine the dimensions in the Golden Mean Ratio chart (right).

GOLDEN MEAN RATIO

If you wish to use the golden mean ratio for your design, use the chart to determine your design's dimensions. If you prefer to figure your own dimensions, do the following:

1. If you know how wide you want your design to be, multiply this width by 1.625 to find your design's length. Example: If you want your design 48″ wide, then multiply 48″ × 1.625 to determine the length (78″). The dimensions are 48″ wide × 78″ long.

2. If you know how long you want your artwork to be, divide it by 1.625 to obtain the width. For example, if you want your design to be 84″ long, divide 1.625 into 84″. The quotient is 51¹¹⁄₁₆″. Rounded up, the dimensions are 52″ wide × 84″ long.

To determine the best ratio for your design's dimensions, look at the seven options on pages 77–81. Which one best suits your design's directional flow and focus? Use the one that makes the most sense for your design. After selecting the ratio, determine one of your design's dimensions. Then figure the other side's dimension by following the ratio guideline. If you decide to work in the 8:13 ratio, see the chart below.

GOLDEN MEAN RATIO

If you want the width to be:	Then the length should be:*	If you want the length to be:	Then the width should be:*
6″	9¾″	6″	3¹¹⁄₁₆″
12″	19½″	12″	7⅜″
18″	29¼″	18″	11¹⁄₁₆″
20″	32½″	20″	12⁵⁄₁₆″
24″	39″	24″	14¾″
30″	48¾″	30″	18½″
36″	58½″	36″	22⅛″
40″	65″	40″	24⅝″
42″	68¼″	42″	25⅞″
45″	73⅛″	45″	27¹¹⁄₁₆″
48″	78″	48″	29½″
50″	81¼″	50″	30¾″
54″	87¾″	54″	33¼″
60″	97½″	60″	36¹⁵⁄₁₆″
66″	107¼″	66″	40⅝″
72″	117″	72″	44⁵⁄₁₆″
78″	126¾″	78″	48″
84″	136½″	84″	51¹¹⁄₁₆″
90″	146¼″	90″	55⅜″
96″	156″	96″	59¹⁄₁₆″
102″	165¾″	102″	62¾″
108″	175½″	108″	66½″
114″	185¼″	114″	70⅛″
120″	195″	120″	73⅞″

Drop the fraction or round up or down to the nearest whole number.

ACTIVITIES AND EXERCISES

1. Look at some of the artwork you have created. Observe each piece from a distance. Are your shapes and objects working together in good proportion (page 74)? If not, what is the problem? How would you resolve the problem if you were to make this design today?

2. With a tape measure or ruler, measure the dimensions of some of your previous artwork. Write down your findings. Next, determine which ratio, if any, you used for each one's dimensions (1:1, 1:2, 1:3, 1:4, 3:4, 2:3, or 8:13) using a calculator (pages 77–81). Write these findings down. Did you find that your dimensions were not based on any ratios? Did you have a habit of choosing one particular ratio for most of your designs? Were you in the habit of selecting ratios with no particular reason or thought? Did you select your dimensions on a whim? Can you see how adjusting the dimensions in some of your designs would increase their beauty?

3. Create three designs that have one shape or object out of proportion. In each design, find a way to make the large shape an integral part of the design.

4. Select three simple designs to play with during the next four weeks: a representational design (page 32), a nonobjective design (page 38), and another design of your choosing. On paper, draw rectangles with the following measurements. Make four copies of each.

2″ × 2″ (1:1 ratio)

2″ × 4″ (1:2 ratio)

2″ × 6″ (1:3 ratio)

2″ × 8″ (1:4 ratio)

3″ × 4″ (3:4 ratio)

2″ × 3″ (2:3 ratio)

4″ × 6½″ or 8″ × 13″ (8:13 ratio)

a. Using a different rectangle each day, draw a version of your representational design in one of the rectangles daily during the first week. Make interesting changes to each of your designs to accommodate each rectangle's dimensions. Try to make each artwork similar to the others but with interesting or pronounced changes to suit the ratio. At week's end, place your representational drawings on a design wall and view them from a distance. Select the designs you like the best and the least. Determine your reasons. What are the dimensions and ratios of your preferred and least favorite designs?

b. Each day of the second week, place your nonobjective design in one of the drawn rectangles. Again, notice how you have to change your design to accommodate the dimensions of each rectangle. Which ratio worked best with your design? Which didn't work at all? What did you find out about working with each ratio? How did you enjoy the process of changing the design to fit the defined dimensions?

c. Each day in the third week, place your doodle design (or other selected design) in a different rectangle. Again, notice how you have to subtly change the design as the design's dimensions change. Which ratios worked best for your design? Which, if any, gave you problems? What did you learn?

d. During the fourth week, make a design specifically for each rectangle. Begin with the same basic idea, but let your imagination play with each. In the end, you will have seven different designs, but they will have a similar starting point, object, or idea. Each will have a different directional flow and focal point.

e. After working with scale during these four weeks, you will have a better feeling for melding a design to its proper scale. From a distance, study your 28 designs. Which designs do you like best? Which ratios did you find were easiest for you to use? Which ratios seemed most difficult to use? Write down your ideas and thoughts. What have you found out about each ratio?

f. Create a new design. Determine its dimensions by using the ratio that allows your design's focus and directional flow to be the most beautiful.

WEEPING WILLOW OVER WATER by Amanda Richardson, Cornwall, England, 102″ × 138″, 2009

Weeping Willow over Water is a commissioned artwork by Amanda Richardson, a renowned textile artist and painter who creates exquisite realistic art based on nature. In this artwork, you see all the design elements come into play beautifully: line, direction, shape, color, value, texture, proportion, and scale. Amanda has blended these elements into this stunning scene through the use of several design principles, including repetition, harmony, unity, and asymmetrical balance. This scene uses an approximate 3:4 ratio. Amanda used silk, polyester, acetate, and cotton in different weaves.

A CITY WALK IN SPRING by Lenore Crawford, Midland, Michigan, 25″ × 38½″, 2008

A City Walk in Spring uses vertical line sublimely. Set in a vertical format, the design shows the reiteration of vertical line in obvious and subtle applications throughout with the couple being the main feature. Texture brings interest and richness to this design. Lenore used fabric, thread, and fabric paint to create this raw-edge fused appliqué.

Photo by Mark Frey, Yelm, Washington

AUTUMN BEAUTY by Barbara Shapel, Washougal, Washington, 56″ × 60″, 2010

The herons and colorful tree are given the majority of visual weight in this autumnal asymmetrical design. Barbara added the sun and the beautiful lustrous sky to create the visual balance on the right side. The textural detailing is elegant in *Autumn Beauty*.

Photo by Gary Silber, Jackson, Mississippi

INFINITY by Gwendolyn A. Magee, Jackson, Mississippi, 90″ × 105″, 1995

For her quilt *Infinity*, Gwendolyn selected a low value key and an analogous color plan. This resulted in a quilt rich in color with beautiful harmony. It is machine pieced and hand quilted.

FEATHERS IN THE WIND by Caryl Bryer Fallert, Paducah, Kentucky, 61″ × 42″, 2010

Feathers in the Wind is a mesmerizing work of art that uses design elements and principles artfully. The horizontal softly curving bands of cool soothing colors are a perfect backdrop for the warm-colored feathers, seemingly swaying in motion. The placement of the feathers allows our eyes to move across the design. There is beautiful unity, variation, contrast, and asymmetrical balance.

Photo by the artist

ORCHID #1 by Annette Kennedy, Longmont, Colorado, 26″ × 21″, 2005

This orchid is a wonderful example of representational realism. Annette's detailing is exquisite in this picture-perfect work of fabric art. A close-up detail can be seen on the front cover of this book.

Photo by the artist

Photo by the artist

DANDELIONS by Frieda L. Anderson, Elgin, Illinois, 50″ × 40″, 2001

Dandelions have never looked happier than in this delightful artwork in which Frieda has used one large dandelion as the main focus and four smaller dandelions to help bring height and visual balance to this asymmetrical design. The border colors and shapes repeat the subtle hues within the main design, allowing our focus to remain on the dandelions.

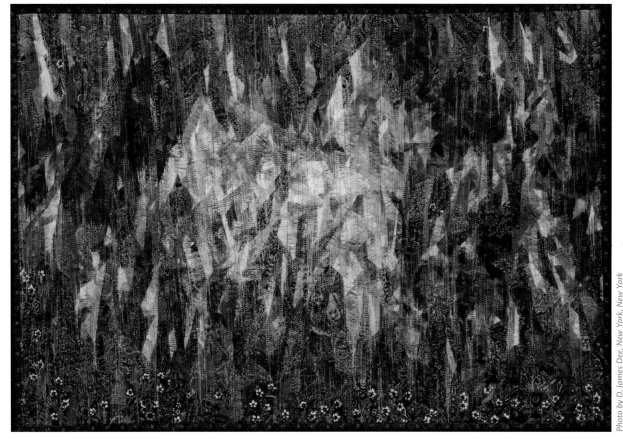

Photo by D. James Dee, New York, New York

SUMMER RAIN by Ludmila Aristova, Brooklyn, New York, 40″ × 28″, 2005

Ludmila's glorious abstract design brings to mind images of summer flowers in the garden after a refreshing rain. The colors vibrate with beauty and movement in this textural delight using nonobjective shapes to create flowers. Also notice the delicately embroidered flowers in the front of the garden. Ludmila used cottons, silk, and ribbons.

FLORAL FORMS I by Judy B. Dales, Greensboro, Vermont, 36″ × 47″, 2006

The beautifully abstracted floral images in this fabric garden are visually provocative, which is one of the great characteristics of representational art in the abstract genre: it encourages us to think, wonder, and be curious. The flowing curves of these flowers move our eyes readily through the design.

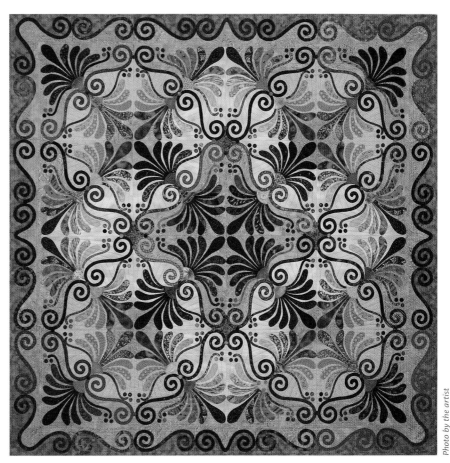

FANDANGO by Rachel Wetzler, St. Charles, Illinois, 68″ × 68″, 2005

Fandango is a fascinating design with wonderful movement, lots of detail, and enticing colors. Because the design radiates outward from the center, it is perfectly balanced. Rachel's beautiful organic shapes draw our eyes into this rhythmic visual dance through repetition, harmony, unity, and contrast.

SOLITUDE BEFORE EIGHT
by Jayne Willoughby Scott,
Edmonton, Alberta, Canada,
30″ × 22″, 2002

This lovely impressionistic scene creates an inviting archway for us to wander through. The defining trees that give clarity and structure to the scene are well placed to help create asymmetrical balance. Jayne used canvas, cheesecloth, velvet, polyester, and thread.

THE GIRLS OF TYRONE FARM by Beth Miller, Kambah, Australian Capital Territory, Australia, 65″ × 45″, 2008

Beth has created such personable girls that this artwork cannot help but put smiles on our faces—particularly for those of us who have fond memories of similar girls. With the use of horizontal line, there is a relaxing quality to this scene. The three cows are positioned for asymmetrical balance; the trees in the background lend contrast to the horizontal elements.

5 OF CLUBS by Irene MacWilliam, Belfast, Northern Ireland, 24″ × 36″, 1998

This fanciful artwork gives us a glimpse into Irene's lively imagination, which is present in many of her artworks. Asymmetrical balance is cleverly attained through the manipulation of the different shapes: the tree and four clubs provide the balance for the golfer. Notice how nonobjective shapes are so cleverly used in this representational design. This artwork uses a 2:3 ratio. *5 of Clubs* was selected to tour the U.K. in the 1998 National Patchwork Association's Deck of 52 Cards exhibit.

DRESDEN FLOWER GARDEN by Judy Simmons, Fletcher, North Carolina, 50″ × 33″, 2007

Judy's adorable design was inspired by the paintings and sketches of Jo Sonja. Fanciful in design style, it is filled with carefree whimsy. The detailing in both flowers and background is wonderful. Our eyes move over the five flowers with ease in this horizontal format. The misty-looking leaves in the background provide interest and invite our eyes to visit this area.

BOXING OUT by Meredith Annett, Halifax, Nova Scotia, Canada, 34″ × 40″, 2004, 2005, 2007

These three geometric boxes are a part of Meredith's *Boxing Out* series of nine boxes. Before Meredith begins a box, she creates a physical model of the box by hand—there is no computer designing in any way. Once she is satisfied with a box's design, Meredith begins her fabric rendition. Each box begins with the same basic size and shape. The different designs are created as Meredith uniquely divides the space, selects shapes, and applies color, value, and texture to create different illusionary effects. Although one box is stunning on its own, *Boxing Out* is an amazing series when seen in full size on a long wall.

THUNDERCLOUDS APPROACHING by Lorraine Torrence, Seattle, Washington; quilted by Jennifer Pielow, Omaha, Nebraska; 56″ × 56″, 2005

Thunderclouds Approaching is striking in its movement of color and value within its square format. The balancing of luminous light-value hues against dark ones is a visual challenge that Lorraine met brilliantly. *Thunderclouds Approaching* was created for Lorraine's book *Shifting Perspectives*.

POULNABRONE DOLMEN by Denise Labadie, Longmont, Colorado, 63″ × 32″, 2008

In the austere land of the Burren in County Clare, Ireland, stands the Poulnabrone Dolmen. Denise has captured the symbolic essence of this megalithic structure magnificently. This artwork is in an approximate 2:1 ratio (pages 77–81).

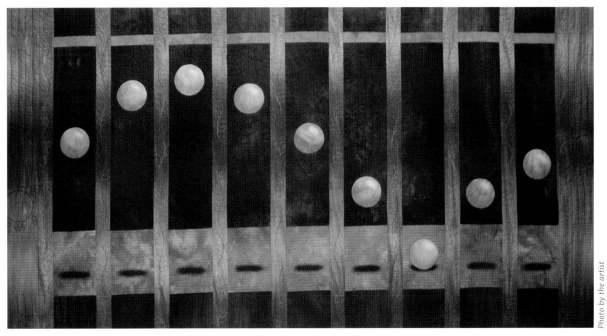

BOUNCE by Colleen Wise, Puyallup, Washington, 60″ × 39″, 2007

Bounce is a great example of how readily our eyes will follow the suggestion of a line—even if it is disconnected. In fact, our eyes are captivated by the suggestion of line. Notice the many ways in which Colleen accentuates horizontal line in this design.

KIMBERLEY MYSTIQUE by Gloria Loughman, Drysdale, Victoria, Australia, 80″ × 88″, 2003

Gloria's *Kimberley Mystique* is surreal in its design style and fabulous in its use of elements and principles. Its surreal trees are awash in amazing colorful textures. Gloria creates her own fabric palette by combining a multitude of fabrics to create glorious textural designs. This artwork is an extraordinary example of the textural possibilities of fabric blending—combining small bits of different fabrics to create a "new" fabric. Gloria used silks, hand-dyed and painted fabrics, and commercial fabrics.

FRAGRANT MEMORIES by Rachel Wetzler, St. Charles, Illinois, 60″ × 51″, 2008

Rachel's attention to detail in this realistic quilt from a past era is incredible—from the rolling pin to the dishcloth, flowers, fruit plate, bread freshly baked, cinnamon rolls ready to be served, wallpaper, outdoor shrubbery … and wood floor. Rachel's excellent fabric selection and placement, along with overlapping, greatly enhance the illusion of depth. *Fragrant Memories* is a warm, comforting visual story that evokes fond memories and happiness. What a treat!

OVERLAY IV: JUNGLE LIGHT by Scott A. Murkin, Asheboro, North Carolina, 52″ × 36″, 2010

Diagonal lines, shining above contrasting light and dark squares, create considerable dynamic energy when color and value move in a playful manner throughout this design's surface. *Overlay IV: Jungle Light* illustrates how effectively you can use line to move color and value.

BIG BANG + 1 SECOND by John Flynn, Billings, Montana, 56″ × 80″, 1994

John's hexagonal spiral design brings into play color, value, line, direction, and texture in innovative ways. John used Lunn Studios' Pointillist Palette fabric, which worked beautifully for the luster and suggestive linear movement. He used a shiny variegated rayon thread on the colorful parts of the quilt, and black thread on the Kona cotton. Notice the subtle diagonal line created through the placement of colors within the blocks. This amazing design uses geometric shapes in a geometric design style. (Acrylic templates are available for this design.)

Photo by the artists

CANTANKEROUS II by Inge Mardal and Steen Hougs, Chantilly, France, 65¾" × 65¾", 2009

Inge Mardal and Steen Hougs, internationally renowned textile artists, create wonderful art that celebrates nature, life, and the art of living. Each year, quilt and textile art connoisseurs await the unveiling of a new and wonderful artwork by this innovative couple. Many of their creations have won prestigious awards in major exhibitions. Each design reveals its own visual story, as you can see by the four designs included in this book. *Cantankerous II* makes me smile, as it reminds me that some birds, like some people, can be very trying on any particular day.

More importantly for us, *Cantankerous II* is alive with design elements and principles: The four background redshanks create repetition, harmony, pattern, and unity. The birds' reflections offer subtle variation while the foreground redshank provides strong contrast. This cantankerous redshank beautifully illustrates the important design principle of contrast—the strongest part of a design often lies in its contrast rather than its repetition. If all five birds were marching in step together, the visual impact would not be the same; nor would it be as interesting. This design causes us to pause, think, and enjoy. (See pages 99 and 119 for related design concepts that this artwork illustrates.)

Each of Inge and Steen's textile artworks provides wonderful examples of nature's elements and principles of design. While you read through the different chapters in this book, I hope you return many times to view *Cantankerous II, The Calm after the Storm, Eye-Catching Eyespot,* and *Tidal Flat* to observe, appreciate, and enjoy the many ways in which Inge and Steen use the elements and principles of design to create their stunning art—there is so much to learn from each piece (above and pages 6, 80, and 104).

Creating the Visual Dance

A BLUEPRINT FOR SUPERB DESIGNS

CHAPTER EIGHT

CREATING STUNNING DESIGNS
with Ten Stellar Principles

The eight elements—line, direction, shape, color, value, texture, proportion, and scale—are the basic ingredients in your design. The way in which you use these elements determines how your design will evolve. You need a plan or a recipe to know how to handle these elemental ingredients. Fortunately, nature provides us with her own set of rules and strategies for creating great designs. This chapter features ten unifying and design-strengthening principles. Most are present in every successful design, while some are used when called upon for specific tasks.

Principle 1: Unity— A Design's Backbone

The backbone of any design is unity. It provides stability and control in the design. It brings visual comfort and clarifies the design. Without unity, visual chaos takes over. Although unity is one of the most important principles, it cannot exist without the help of other closely related principles. Repetition is the major principle of choice to create unity. However, other principles can play a role too. Use your imagination to select the ancillary principles that will promote the unity your design requires.

Principles 2, 3, and 4: Repetition, Rhythm, and Harmony

Repetition creates unity. Repetition in design is simply repeating one or more elements. Every element does not need to be repeated. If too many elements are repeated, predictability, visual monotony, and disinterest can result. Every artwork in this chapter features at least one repeating element that serves to create unity. Your personality often dictates your use of repetition. If you prefer well-organized, structured designs, the number of elements repeated may be much higher than if you have more free-spirited organizational habits.

The principle of repetition is very versatile. It not only promotes the existence of unity, but it plays a significant role in the appearances of the principles of rhythm and harmony. Repetition that flows fluidly throughout a design allows rhythm to come forth. When repetition and rhythm work together in a visually pleasing manner, harmony is created.

Fiesta uses the principle of repetition well by repeating squares, colors, and curved lines. This repetition provides a sense of rhythm. The principles are presented in such a manner that harmony exists. *Ogenblik (Twinkling of an Eye)* uses different repeated objects to create repetition, rhythm, and harmony (page 98). Observe the use of repetition, rhythm, and harmony in *Luminosity* and *Along the Winner Creek Trail* (pages 45 and 98). Notice that each of these designs has unity.

FIESTA by Norma Schlager, Danbury, Connecticut, 58″ × 58″, 2008

Fiesta's unity has been created through repetition of the squares, colors, and the free-form curved shapes. Subtle value change between the squares creates interesting contrast, as the lightest squares act as the border while the darkest ones create a central focus.

OGENBLIK (TWINKLING OF AN EYE) by Ans Kastein, Didam, the Netherlands, 37½″ × 47¼″, 2008

Ans's nonobjective artwork was inspired by the works of Gustav Klimt. The triangles unify the major section of this design while repetitious eyes unify the narrow left side with the right side. Other design features, such as the background curving squiggles and the small triangles, provide subtle repetitive variation.

Photo by Photostudio Marks, Didam, the Netherlands

Lack of unity is one of the major reasons a design is unsuccessful. Too much variety creates visual chaos. If no repetition exists, there is nothing to hold the design together. Its haphazard appearance leaves the eye wondering where to look. Determine what will provide the repetition needed to create unity. Enhance your design further by promoting rhythm and harmony.

ALONG THE WINNER CREEK TRAIL by Linda Beach, Chugiak, Alaska, 68″ × 39″, 2005

This luscious scene brings thoughts of autumn's arrival with its analogous coloring. Unity is created through repetition of the yellow-toned leaves. Variation and interest are provided by the size, shape, and color changes of the leaves. The dark tree trunks in the background present a rich contrast to the warm leaves in this beautiful woodland scene. The leaves play a dominant role, so there is no conflict in where our eyes will rest.

Photo by Danny Daniels, Anchorage, Alaska

Principles 5 and 6: Variation and Contrast

Although unity is essential in a design's success, too much unity can cause monotony and predictability. This brings us to another important design principle: *Variation or contrast with unity creates a stronger design than unity alone.* Variety creates increased interest in a design. However, the design's interest is strongest where contrast exists and the unity is broken.

Galaxy is a beautifully patterned design showing unity through repetition. Rhythm and harmony are also present.

Variation is added through the shifting motif shapes. This design's greatest strength, however, lies where its contrast is strongest—in the orange four-pointed star. This is another excellent example of the fact that our eyes are most interested in the place where the pattern is interrupted. *Floating Frames* (page 100) uses square frames to create unity but then provides variation and contrast through value, color, and size. Bags and pipes are the primary unifying factor in *Bagpipes* (page 105).

GALAXY by John Flynn, Billings, Montana, 31″ × 41″, 2003

Galaxy is an excellent example of repetition, rhythm, harmony, and unity. Variation has been created by the curved motif changing as it is stretched and squeezed in its block form. The greatest interest in this design, however, lies where the pattern is interrupted and the contrast is strongest—the orange four-pointed star. The 3:4 ratio selected is perfect for this design (pages 77–81). (Laser-cut acrylic templates are available for this design.)

Cantankerous II (page 95) is a splendid example of variation and contrast combining with unity to make a stronger design. The four redshanks all walking in the same direction create unity through repetition. The foremost redshank, standing tall and facing a different direction, provides contrast. The subtle differences in the redshanks' steps and shadows provide variation. Inge Mardal and Steen Hougs have made this a strong, interesting design because they used contrast and variation with unity. Notice that your eyes are most attracted to where the pattern of repetition has been broken—the cantankerous bird, not the four amicable ones. This illustrates well that the strength of a design lies in the contrast, not in the repetition. That being said, the design needs its repetitive features to create unity.

FLOATING FRAMES by Bill Horn, Austin, Texas, 64" × 64", 2008

This quilt illustrates great use of repetition, rhythm, harmony, and unity, as square frames are magically placed throughout the design. Variation and contrast are incorporated through changes in the frames' colors, values, and sizes. This design is enhanced by the textures used in both the frames and the background. Luster, created through value change, enriches the design brilliantly. Using the brightest and most pronounced colorations for the foreground and the most subdued in the receding frames creates a wonderful sense of dimensionality. *Floating Frames* is perfectly balanced and well placed in a 1:1 ratio (page 77). (See page 110 for further discussion about this design.)

African Dreams and *Nest III* are rhythmic in their repetition of shapes and flowing movement. In the former, the black ovals provide contrast; in the latter, the large orange-red nucleus creates contrast. The cellular shapes in *Cellular Structure VIII (Oval Shift)* (page 31) provide visual organization and unity. The background colors create contrast and the painterly squiggles create wonderful variation.

Contrast Is Powerful

REMEMBER: A design's strength is rarely found in its repetitious pattern. Instead, the most powerful and interesting area in a design is the area that visually interrupts the repetitious pattern—where the strongest contrast exists.

AFRICAN DREAMS by Gloria Loughman, Drysdale, Victoria, Australia, 38″ × 49″, 2008

African Dreams is filled with beautiful textures and free-flowing shapes that provide repetition and unity. The five blackened ovals provide contrast and give our eyes a place to focus. *African Dreams* includes beautiful value shifts in this analogous color plan.

Photo by Anthony Loughman, Drysdale, Victoria, Australia

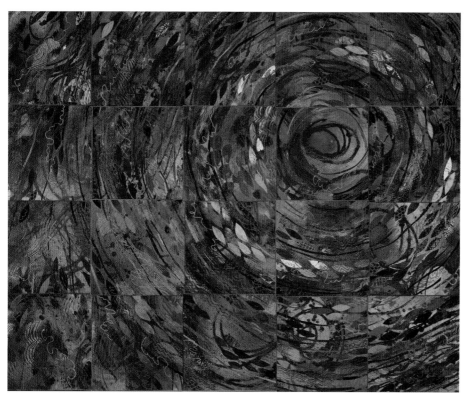

NEST III by Sue Benner, Dallas, Texas, 77½″ × 62″, 2002

Repetition of shapes, direction, texture, and color create wonderful rhythm and harmony in *Nest III*. This results in beautiful movement and unity in this nonobjective design. The large orange circular shape presents contrast and a place for the eye to rest. This design uses the rule-of-thirds focus structure for its balance, with the large contrasting orange shape placed within the upper right intersecting point (page 117).

Photo by John Lanning, Raleigh, North Carolina

The guitar shapes in *Groovy Guitars* provide unity; the change of color and value adds contrast and variation to the design. The tree trunks in *Setting Sun, Rising Moon* offer excellent repetition, which provides unity in this design; the trunks' hues provide interesting variation. The moon also offers contrast. *Forbidden Fruit* is a strongly patterned design created through the repetition of shape, value, and color. Our eyes are riveted to the strongly contrasting image—the apple, which is the highlight of the design.

SETTING SUN, RISING MOON by Linda Beach, Chugiak, Alaska, 60″ × 36″, 2009

In this lovely evening scene the tree trunks offer excellent repetition, which provides soothing unity in this design. The trunks' hues offer interesting variation. The moon furnishes visual contrast. Linda used an approximate golden mean ratio (1:1.625; see pages 77–81).

Photo by Danny Daniels, Anchorage, Alaska

FORBIDDEN FRUIT by Anna Faustino, Tobyhanna, Pennsylvania, 41½″ × 41½″, 2004

Forbidden Fruit is a dramatic eye-catcher! The unity in this design is created by the repetition of beautiful warm analogous orange-gold shapes offset by black and charcoal shapes. The solitary apple with its trio of leaves provides a striking contrast to the overall pattern. Anna subtly changed both value and color as she moved from the black border to the center. Value plays an important role in allowing the apple to take center stage without having any competition between it and the background shapes.

GROOVY GUITARS by Robbi Joy Eklow, Third Lake, Illinois, 40″ × 54″, 2003

Robbi Joy's design was inspired by Gustav Klimt. The gathering of guitars offers repetition, which provides harmony, rhythm, and unity. The guitars vary in their shapes. The warm green set against the dominant browns and oranges creates eye-catching visual contrast.

Principle 7: Bridging

The principle of *bridging* can play a strong role in creating unity. Visual extremes are difficult for the eye to accept. Bridging is used to gently move from one extreme to another. For instance, the seasons of spring and fall are the natural bridges between summer and winter. Bridging is used most often with color, value, and shape.

Color is a great element for bridging when combining two colors. Four gradation bridges using variations of yellow and violet are shown here.

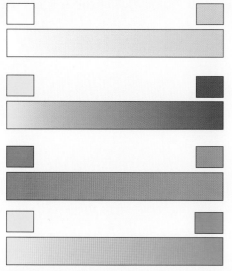

Bridging lessens the impact of extreme differences in color or intensity.

An example of bridging color through gradation can be seen in *Dream of Infinity* (below and page 4). Other examples are *Pizzazz* and *Autumn Beauty* (background) (pages 43 and 85).

Value is one of the most exciting elements to use in bridging. Moving value from light to dark can add great drama to a design. Also, it captivates the eye. Bridging value is easy to do and its effect can be stunning.

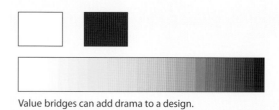

Value bridges can add drama to a design.

There are many examples of bridging through value in this book, including *Northern Lights, Luminosity, Moonlight Sonata,* and *Unnamed Log Cabin* (pages 20, 45, 49, and 126). Another example is *Ma, How Come She Gets All the Attention?*

Photo by Mark Frey, Yelm, Washington

MA, HOW COME SHE GETS ALL THE ATTENTION?
by Helen Remick, Seattle, Washington, 56″ × 62″, 2004

Helen used value as a bridge to create this lustrous background. This bridge accentuates her beautifully dimensional star.

DREAM OF INFINITY
by Dineke Ugen, Roden, the Netherlands, 39″ × 39″, 2006

Dineke used bridging to move color in her design. The square format accentuates the premier role of the circular motif.

Photo by Ruud Ugen

Bridging large and small shapes through size gradation is very compelling. It offers an interesting way to play with design.

Bridging different shapes through gradation works very well, as it allows the eye to move with the objects.

Fibonacci's Garden (page 76) is a beautiful example of bridging shapes from large to small. *Enchanted Journey* (page 75) uses a more informal bridging approach.

Another way to use gradation with shapes is to change the shapes subtly as they move across the design surface.

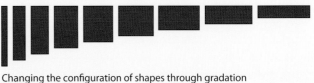

Changing the configuration of shapes through gradation works very well in a design, as it allows the eye to move through the design.

Don't Bug Me (page 37) changes shapes very cleverly in its design. Notice how effectively Anna Faustino used value too.

If you have an area in your design with little or no detail, consider bridging through gradation of color and/or value there to create interest and balance in your design. Find effective ways to use bridging. Not only will this principle create an interesting way to provide unity, it will enhance your design immeasurably. *Autumn Beauty* and *Poulnabrone Dolmen* (pages 85 and 91) do this brilliantly, as does *Tidal Flat.*

Photo by the artists

TIDAL FLAT by Inge Mardal and Steen Hougs, Chantilly, France, 73½″ × 55½″, 2003

Tidal Flat offers unexpected visual pleasure through this design's value placement, with the strong dark values in the upper part of the design and the light ones below. The result is strikingly evocative. Bridging the two value extremes here is done beautifully. The use of proximity with the three ringed plovers provides unity in this marvelous scene. This design uses a 4:3 ratio (pages 77–81).

Principle 8: Proximity

One very simple way to create unity is to use the principle of *proximity*. When you are planning your design, make certain the objects in your design are close enough that they have a visual bond—a visual relationship. Objects need to be in close proximity for unity. You can see this principle clearly in the illustrations below. The pieces of fruit in the first image are isolated. The design feels disjointed; it lacks unity. In the second image, the pieces of fruit are in close proximity. There is a visual relationship, which results in unity. Isn't it amazing how different seven pieces of fruit can look simply due to proximity or the lack of it?

A lack of proximity can create a disjointed design with no unity.

Proximity provides a visual relationship that creates unity.

Tidal Flat (page 104) illustrates proximity beautifully. The three ringed plovers, standing in the tidal flat close together, are bonded together visually. This close proximity creates unity. If Inge Mardal and Steen Hougs had placed these three ringed plovers far from each other, so that each was isolated, there would be no visual bonding. Our eyes would flit from one bird to the other, not knowing where to rest. The design would be disjointed. Because they placed the birds together, our eyes go right to them. This brings beautiful unity to the image.

Pamela Mostek uses the principle of proximity very well to create unity in *Five Apples* (page 7). In *Reflections* (page 33) the three rounded trees clumped together create unity. You can see how important proximity can be in certain designs. The swimming objects in *A Dream of Swimming Points* (page 63) almost touch each other as they circle around the center. Because they are in close proximity, unity prevails. In *Bagpipes*, Judy Simmons gave herself a challenge by isolating the five bags. Notice the pattern of notes and circles Judy used to lead our eyes from one bag to another. This repetition, along with the subtle diagonal line, leads to visual bonding. You will find numerous examples of the principle of proximity throughout this book. Notice the different ways people use this principle.

BAGPIPES by Judy Simmons, Fletcher, North Carolina, 31″ × 37″, 2007

Bagpipes is a very clever fanciful design! The development of unity was essential since the five bags and their pipes are isolated spatially. To create this unity, Judy used colors in each bag that related to the others. Her border treatment enhances unity. In addition, Judy provided small circles and notes for visual pathways, so our eyes could move easily from one area to another. Judy used an uneven number of bags and pipes in this design, so our eyes can find a place to rest. She used printed images, piping, and decorative threads for this artwork.

Photo by Tim Barnwell, Asheville, North Carolina

Principle 9: Movement

Repeating an object or shape across the design surface creates unity. Because the eye moves along the pathway of these objects, it appears to create movement. Visual movement can be provocative, challenging, and exciting.

Caryl Bryer Fallert's *High Tech Tucks #35* creates unity through movement as it moves our eyes across the design. The circles in *Fibonacci's Garden* (page 76) move our eyes upward throughout the design.

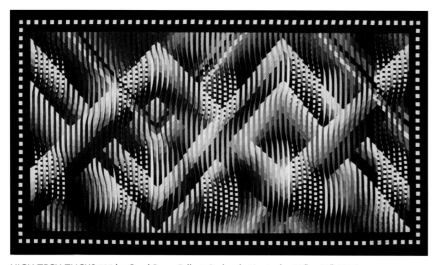

HIGH TECH TUCKS #35 by Caryl Bryer Fallert, Paducah, Kentucky, 79″ × 44″, 1994

A master colorist, Caryl's fabric art flows with stunning colors. This energizing design entices our eyes to wander across the artwork with intense interest.

Photo by the artist

As illustrated in *Bounce* (page 91), it's not necessary to have an unbroken line engage our eyes for movement to exist. Our eyes are curious. They take visual suggestion quite readily—including movement. In *Moonlight Sonata* (page 49), our eyes follow the suggestive diagonal line, moving from the herons' lower bodies upward to the moon. In *Eye-Catching Eyespot* (page 80), our eyes move in a diagonal fashion because the subtle line leads the way—even though the line is broken, our eyes know where to go. Knowing that our eyes take suggestion well is a great design tip.

Principle 10: Dominance

With the principle of *dominance,* one element plays the dominant role in a design. This enhances visual unity. It makes perfect sense if you think about it. You have eight players on your design team: *line, direction, shape, color, value, texture, proportion,* and *scale.* Without a plan, it's easy for one element to take over the design without consent. Or, perhaps two elements vie for equal attention, thereby creating conflict and confusion. They can't all be the leader. If every element tried to take the dominant position, you'd have visual chaos.

Establish which element will be your lead player. It will have the dominant role. Select another element to play the secondary role. You may want another element or two to play lesser roles, giving visual support to your design.

Sticking to Your Principles

Once you are clear as to which elements will play the major and secondary roles in your design, your ideas will begin falling into place. Which principles do you really like? Determine how you will create unity, contrast, and variation in this design. Then begin playing. As your design develops, stand back often to assess its progress. If there's not enough unity, add more repetition. If there is too much unity, find a way to bring in additional contrast or variation. If your design lacks interest, consider using additional principles, such as bridging or movement. Use these ten great principles to your advantage to create magical designs.

ACTIVITIES AND EXERCISES

1. Look for patterns in nonartistic objects around your home. Seek 25 different patterns created from repetition of one or more design elements. If some excite or inspire you, draw them in your design notebook or journal or take digital pictures of them.

2. Create one small design for each of the following principles:

- Unity through repetition, rhythm, and harmony

- Unity with variation and contrast

- Bridging extremes through gradation

- Unity through proximity

- Unity through movement

3. In each of the following twelve days, create one small design using paints, fabric, paper, colored paper, or any other medium. Using index cards, your design notebook, or other paper, do the following:

a. On the first day, select one of *line, color, value,* or *texture* to play the dominant role in the first part of this exercise. Next, choose another of these elements to play the secondary role. Create a design using these elements in the two strongest roles. Other elements should be present in your design too. Make certain there are unity, contrast, and variation in the design.

b. On the second day, repeat the exercise with line, color, value, or texture as the same dominant element, but select a different element to play the secondary role. Make a design using these two elements in the leading roles. Adapt your design to work well with your new secondary element. (This design can be similar to your first design or it can be different.)

c. Repeat the same exercise twice more, using your originally chosen dominant element, but combine it with each of the remaining two elements, using them in a secondary role.

d. Create one design each of the following days, rotating the four elements so that each element has the opportunity to play the dominant role with each of the other three elements in a secondary role.

e. Look at your twelve designs. Which combinations did you most enjoy working with? Which led to the most interesting designs? Which combinations were the most difficult for you to work with? Which element would you like to use as the dominant element in your next design? Which element would you like to partner with it as the secondary element?

4. Go to galleries and museums to observe the artwork. Choose about twelve artworks that you like and six that you don't care for. In all, observe what is dominant in the designs. Was there any artwork that didn't appear to show dominance? If so, how did you like these designs? Look through a few art books and do the same analysis.

5. If you love the idea of using suggestive line to create unity through movement, look through the artwork to find other examples that move your eye through the design. Notice how it is done. Create your own design using the principle of movement.

CHAPTER NINE

THE BALANCING ACT
Creating Visual Balance *with* Two Superb Principles

When you see a beautiful work of art, you enjoy it. As you stand there admiring it, you're not thinking about shape, value, color, focus, dominance, unity, or balance. None of those concepts registers in your mind. You are looking at the art as a whole, not its parts. That is because everything works. The artist has made a visual statement using nature's design elements and principles. In essence, the artist has created a beautiful, rhythmic *visual dance.*

Creating our own visual dance is what we strive for when we begin a design. We want to be excited about our designs when we have completed them, and we want others to enjoy and be excited about them too. You have at your fingertips the ingredients for this visual dance—the elements of design—but two very important principles are still left to explore. This chapter delves into nature's remaining principles: balance and focus. These concepts are the crème de la crème of design.

Principle 11: Balance

SYMMETRICAL BALANCE

Classical architecture with its graceful, elegant lines is based on symmetry. So are many beautiful works of art. A symmetrical design is organized, harmonic, and well balanced. We will discuss three different types of symmetrical designs: radiating outward from a center point, bilateral mirror-image reflections, and axes and quadrants. They all provide controlled, perfectly weighted symmetrical balance.

Radial Balance—Circular Designs

Radial design is an exquisite form of symmetry. The balance is beautifully controlled in a design that moves around a center point. Most radial designs are circular in nature, but some simply imply circular energy, as their designs radiate around their centers. Radial balance is used in nature in thousands of examples—a simple dandelion, a frilly peony, a luscious rose. ...

PINEAPPLE SURPRISE AGAIN
by Judy Spiers, Foxworth, Mississippi, 19½″ × 19½″, 2006

This exquisite miniature Pineapple Log Cabin quilt is based on radial balance. It is a replica of Judy's award-winning quilt that is owned by the Museum of the American Quilter's Society.

A stone dropped into a pond shows radial balance. A slice of a cucumber, carrot, or tomato offers radial balance. *Pineapple Surprise Again* shows radial balance. Additional examples include *Cheddar Cheese, Primrose, Amazon Star, Sedona, Rosa Celeste,* and *Bright Hopes* (pages 21, 37, 58, 59, 70, and 138).

Most radial designs are circular in nature, but some imply circular energy, as their design radiates around their centers, as seen in this rose.

Bilateral Symmetry—
Balance with a Mirror Image

Bilateral symmetry can be quite beautiful and evocative. One half of the design reflects the other. The two sides are mirror images of each other. People, animals, and many other living creatures are bilaterally symmetrical. Often we see bilateral symmetry in exact duplication, particularly in art.

Bilateral symmetry: Ballet of Iris

There is no requirement that the mirror-image sides be absolutely identical (think of the subtle differences in people's faces). As long as the weight and structure are similar, there can be differences within the two sides. We see a relaxing of expectations when bilateral symmetry occurs in natural settings such as reflections.

Bilateral symmetry: Reflections on water can create a mirror image.

Tsunami (page 23) is a stunning example of bilateral symmetry. Other bilaterally symmetrical designs include *Haight Fantasy* and *Jessica's Flower Basket.*

HAIGHT FANTASY by Gloria Hansen, East Windsor, New Jersey, 16″ × 22″, 2003

Haight Fantasy is a beautiful example of bilateral symmetry. The left side is a mirror image of the right side. In addition, in this design the top half is a mirror image of the bottom half. This design is well suited for a rectangular format because the central star design has been elongated. Gloria used gradual value change to create luster in selected areas.

JESSICA'S FLOWER BASKET by Sue Nickels, Ann Arbor, Michigan, 28″ × 28″, 2007

Jessica's Flower Basket is an excellent example of bilateral symmetry using a formal design such as this: the left side is identical to the right side. Texture plays a secondary role in *Jessica's Flower Basket* with the elegant quilting stitches Sue designed for this quilt. (Pattern is available.)

Quilts such as *Ticonderoga Star, New Beginnings,* and *Bear Tracks in the Garden* have two different balancing acts going on in their designs (pages 78, 130, and 135). The individual blocks that make up the overall design are based on symmetry using axes and quadrants (page 110). However, the overall designs are placed in a bilaterally symmetrical setting.

Symmetry: Using Perpendicular Axes and Quadrants

Many symmetrical designs are based on perpendicular axes and their quadrants. Each quadrant is a mirror image of its neighboring quadrants. The four quadrants within the design provide a stable, balanced structure. Most geometric quilt blocks are based on this type of symmetry.

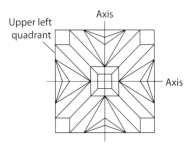

Most geometric quilt blocks are based on symmetry using perpendicular axes and their quadrants.

Many historically styled designs use the symmetry of axes and quadrants. *Northern Lights* is based on this symmetry. Other examples include *Tropical Radiance, Fantasia, Fandango,* and *Perspectives II* (pages 10, 45, 87, and 126).

Floating Frames (page 100) is intriguing with its numerous squares of different sizes, colors, and planes. It looks quite complex in its makeup. If you look at the design, the quadrants do not appear identical, yet the design is beautifully balanced. Rotate the design 45° so you see the design on its diagonal. Now you can see how perfectly balanced it is; one diagonal side is a mirror image of the other. *Floating Frames* is an excellent example of creating dimensionality on a flat surface.

If you wish to achieve controlled balance that offers beautiful designs, use symmetrical balance in your designs. It will be uncomplicated and give you good, predictable results no matter whether the symmetry is radial, bilateral, or based on perpendicular axes and quadrants.

Photo by Chris Reardon, Halifax, Nova Scotia, Canada

NORTHERN LIGHTS by Meredith Annett, Halifax, Nova Scotia, Canada, 48″ × 48″, 1994

Meredith created this symmetrical design using perpendicular axes and four quadrants, which provides beautiful symmetry. *Northern Lights* illustrates the use of dark-value hues in a low-key design. This design works very well because enough value contrast is present to allow viewers to see the design from a distance. Meredith enhanced her design further by creating luminosity with warm, clear middle-value reds surrounded by slightly toned hues.

ASYMMETRICAL BALANCE

Asymmetrical design is the most difficult of all balance structures. If you have not been privy to its design secrets, you can easily become frustrated working in asymmetrical balance. So this section is devoted to delving into the mysteries of asymmetrical design—and decreasing your stress level when designing.

There are many useful tips to help us create balance in our asymmetrical designs. The balance rule that most people know is the *uneven rule.* Simply put, using an uneven number of objects in a grouping, such as 1, 3, 5, or 7, allows our eyes the ability to find an object on which to rest. When an even number of objects is present, our eyes don't know what to focus on, so they flit back and forth, never resting. This results in visual discomfort. There are exceptions to this rule, but when in doubt use an uneven number of objects.

Unbridled Passion (one lady) and *Yellow Daisies* (three daisies) show good balance with their uneven groupings (pages 118 and 119). *Friends in High Places* contains one balloon and three flowers. Other examples include *Five Apples, Feathers in the Wind, The Girls of Tyrone Farm, Dresden Flower Garden,* and *Tidal Flat* (pages 7, 85, 88, 89, and 104). *A City Walk in Spring* (page 84) illustrates an important exception to the rule: Our eyes view two people together as a couple—a group of one. This natural blending doesn't happen with two balls or two flowers, but it does happen with two people.

Photo by Ken Wagner, Seattle, Washington

FRIENDS IN HIGH PLACES by Mickey Depre, Oak Lawn, Illinois, 19¼″ × 26¾″, 2007

In this fanciful design, Mickey used an uneven number of flowers to create the main focus. One flower was given visual prominence in size and color. These three flowers form a well-balanced unit. Additionally, Mickey added the red balloon to provide the balance needed for this vertical format. The balloon's size, color, and placement all were important factors in providing balance. The balloon also helps move the eye upward through the design. (Pattern is available.)

Interestingly, gravity can play an allusive role in asymmetrical design. We expect heavy objects and dark colors (low values) to be placed in a design's lower section. Conversely, light-value objects and colors are expected to be in the upper region of a design. In fact, we are taken by surprise when the law of gravity is overruled in a design. That being said, it is *not* incorrect to put heavy shapes or dark colors in the top portion of a design; nor is it wrong to place light objects or light colorings in the bottom region. When it is done, our eyes are riveted to that design because it is so unexpected—and usually quite exciting. Such is the case in *Tidal Flat* (page 104). The unexpected placement of dark and light gives the design strong visual power. As Inge Mardal and Steen Hougs did with this artwork, dare to do the unexpected if it makes sense in your design.

Strategies for Visual Weight Control

When one side of a design has more visual weight than the other side, the design is unbalanced.

To help disperse visual weight, a large shape should move closer to the design's vertical center while a small object should move farther from the center on the opposite side.

A large object's heaviness on one side can be counterbalanced by several small objects placed on the other side of the vertical center.

Visual weight can be changed within a design by manipulating color and value, by making intensity changes in colors, by varying the sizes of shapes, by varying the detail or complexity of the shapes, by varying the number of shapes, and by repositioning shapes.

Here are some weight-manipulation guidelines to keep in mind when working with asymmetry:

- A large shape weighs more than a small shape.

- A dark object weighs more than a light one when both are the same size.

- A shape near a perimeter edge is more attractive to our eyes than if the same shape is positioned near the vertical center.

- A small colorful object can weigh as much as a large subtly colored object because our eyes are attracted to color.

- A small intricate object can weigh as much as a large plain object because our eyes are attracted to detail and complexity.

Keeping the above information in mind, consider the following:

- *To give more visual weight to an object,* you can increase the size of the object, increase the intensity of the object's color, darken the value of the object, and/or make the object more detailed or more complex.

- *To lighten the visual weight,* you can make the object smaller, use a grayer (more toned) color, lighten the object's value, and/or make the object less detailed.

If you need to reposition one or more objects on one or both sides, consider the following:

- The farther an object is placed from the center and the more isolated that object is, the more it weighs and the more it attracts the eye.

- A large object close to the center can be balanced by a small object placed farther away on the opposite side.

- An isolated object weighs more in an open space than it would if the object were among several objects.

Oak Veiling, Sisters on the Heath, and *Moon Dance* illustrate several of these strategies, as does *Fishermen's Widows* (page 114).

OAK VEILING by Linda Beach, Chugiak, Alaska, 47″ × 47″, 2009

Linda challenged herself by placing this beautiful asymmetrical tree in a square format (1:1 ratio, page 77). She had to place the tree on the left side of the imaginary centerline to achieve balance. The three small tree trunks on the right side, along with the light sky behind, help counterbalance the substantial tree trunk and abundant branches.

SISTERS ON THE HEATH by Kay D. Haerland,
Green Point, New South Wales, Australia, 36½″ × 24½″, 2007

In this lovely scene, the sisters play an important role in distributing visual weight with their dark coats and colorful umbrellas. The left side of the scene is darker and has more strongly placed objects than the right side. The sister with the red umbrella provides a colorful focus on this side. Placing the two sisters with their colorful umbrellas between the two trees on the right forms a visual alliance, which equalizes the weight and creates interest on that side. Kay used cotton, tulle, lamé, velvet, Ultrasuede, lace, and wool strands.

MOON DANCE by Annette Kennedy, Longmont, Colorado, 29″ × 21″, 2009

Moon Dance is an asymmetrical design that creates its balance through the distribution of visual weight. The moon and the solitary lone squiggly whitish line on the right side of the vertical centerline provide the visual weight needed to balance the multitude of dark lines on the left side.

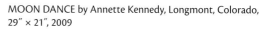

FISHERMEN'S WIDOWS by Anna Faustino, Tobyhanna, Pennsylvania, 41½″ × 61″, 2008

In *Fishermen's Widows*, Anna had to contend with the difficult balance challenges that often plague asymmetrical designs. Anna had to find ways to entice our eyes to move away from the large building on the left, which carries considerable visual weight. Up for the task, Anna found ways to create a balanced scene that would move our eyes through the design.

In the upper right quadrant, Anna placed strongly colored water, the sky with its soft reiteration of the water color, and a dark green woodland. In the bottom of that quadrant, the two women with their dark clothes are great attractions. In the bottom right quadrant, Anna provides interest with a well-placed lustrous white gull. Adding mauve hues to the stones and a horizontal shadow line increases the interest. As Anna hoped, our eyes move through this asymmetrical scene because she has created interest throughout.

The Balancing Act

With the heron placed in the vertical center spot, almost all the weight in this design is on the right side. This creates an unbalanced design.

If the heron is placed at the left edge of the design, the weight is placed on the left side, resulting in an unbalanced design.

By placing an imaginary vertical line through the design's center, we can position the heron so its weight is equally distributed on each side of the vertical center. If it seems impossible to distribute the weight evenly, add one or more small objects on the side that needs a bit more weight.

When working on an asymmetrical design, I suggest that you divide your design in half with an imaginary vertical centerline. This line will provide you information that can help distribute the weight throughout the design. In an asymmetrical design, there should be enough interest on both sides of the design to draw your eyes across the vertical centerline at least once. Additionally, there should be a similar amount of visual weight on the left side as on the right. If there is no reason for the eye to venture to the other side, you'll have to determine what to do to bring interest to that side.

To experiment, place an imaginary vertical centerline on the tree reflection image below. Do your eyes want to cross from one side to the other? Is there similar weight on both sides? If your answer is no to either question, determine what changes you could make if this were your work of art.

Now, place an imaginary horizontal centerline through the same image. Look at each quadrant. Is there something of interest in each quadrant to attract your eye? It doesn't have to be an object that captures your interest in a quadrant. You can use interesting textures, color changes, or value changes as important design elements to help distribute visual weight and create interest to draw the eye. If there is a problem with one or more quadrants, decide what it is and how it can be fixed.

Using imaginary vertical and horizontal centerlines to assess both interest and weight

When working on an asymmetrical design, first concentrate on getting the weight distributed on the left and right sides. Then draw the imaginary horizontal line to see how each quadrant is holding its own weight. If you find that a quadrant has considerable open space but little interest, think about gradating values or colors to create the interest needed for the eye to want to visit that quadrant.

Look at the photos of the quilts mentioned on the next page. Place the imaginary vertical and horizontal centerlines on the designs to better understand what led their creators to choose the selected strategy.

In *Lakeside* (page 63), the weight of the large tree is balanced by the dark land on the left side, as well as the gradation of value and subtle color change in the lake and the sky. This gradation keeps our eyes interested in the left side of the design.

In *Interwoven*, the foreground tree was placed as close to the perimeter edge as possible. This accentuates this tree's power over all the other trees. If Linda Beach had wanted the tree to be de-emphasized, she would have moved the tree toward the centerline. The background trees counterbalance the powerful foreground tree.

INTERWOVEN by Linda Beach, Chugiak, Alaska, 59" × 39", 2009

Interwoven is a splendid example of strong value contrast—high and low (light/dark). These beautiful gnarly trees stand boldly in this design because of the extreme value contrast. The darkened trees set against the softened light backdrop are powerful in their striking beauty.

Photo by Danny Daniels, Anchorage, Alaska

In *Weeping Willow over Water* (page 83), Amanda Richardson selected beautiful, bright blue water with lovely textures to capture our eyes' attention in the bottom right quadrant. The combination of eye-catching water and tall flowers provides the visual weight to balance the bottom section of this design with the stunning weeping willow.

Landscape images can be asymmetrical challenges, but they give us an excellent opportunity to practice our weight-distribution skills. The image of the sunset in the Smoky Mountains (above right) provides a particularly intriguing weight-distribution challenge. Mesmerized by the glorious sunset, I found my design options bleak with a dark hill that refused to move. This is a good image to use to add more skills to our asymmetrical toolbox.

Visual weight distribution challenge

First, place an *imaginary* line at the vertical center to see what's happening on both sides of the design. Do you find interest on both sides? Do the sun and sky on the left counterbalance the large dark hill on the right? Now, add an imaginary horizontal line. Look at each quadrant. What problems do you see? How would you deal with the unequal weight if this were your design?

If it appears impossible to create interest in all four quadrants or to attain good visual weight distribution in a design, one useful design-element option is ready to go to work—scale (page 77). Sometimes changing a design's scale will allow everything to fall into place. If we change the scale in the Smoky Mountains sunset image, the image will be smaller. However, there has to be some manipulation of the dimensions, so the ratio (page 77) will change. To experiment, first cut four fat strips of paper to use as framing perimeter lines. Place the strips on the image and play with them until you think you have a pleasing, balanced image. You can make the image narrower or shorter than the original, you can make the image a vertical format, or you can make it a narrow horizontal image. Determine the best ratio for a vertical format with the sun on the vertical centerline. Also, see if you can make a good horizontal image.

Making the design surface smaller or larger (changing the scale) can be a simple solution to a design problem. Changing the dimensional ratio can work wonders too. If you are frustrated with a design, and manipulating shapes, values, and colors doesn't seem to work, think about changing the scale and/or changing the dimensional ratio.

Principle 12: Focus

The area you want our eyes to gravitate to first should be the most defined area of your design. You create focus by establishing the difference between the featured shape and its setting. That can be accomplished by making the shape a brighter color, a different color, a lighter or darker color, a different shape, or a more textured shape. In other words, you need to provide a variation in order for our eyes to be attracted to the focus area. If the focus is too similar to its surroundings in color and/or value, our eyes won't see it.

USING A FOCUS STRUCTURE

It is helpful to have a structure from which to build your design. This structure is much like a body's skeleton. It holds everything together. Without structure, the design can feel disjointed. Your design's structure will attract the eye and guide it toward the design's featured area or main focus. Several design structures are discussed below.

Rule of Thirds

The *rule of thirds* is an easy way to find a focus range. Simply divide your design into thirds, horizontally and vertically. Four intersecting points will appear. Place your featured focus in the vicinity of the most appropriate intersecting point.

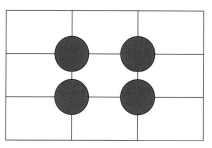

The rule of thirds: an easy strategy for positioning a focus in the design

The wind-blown pansy has to be the main focus in the photo, because it is the most outstanding object in this image. It needs to have a placement that provides good asymmetrical balance. Using the rule of thirds is the perfect strategy for this image. The only intersecting point that could be considered is the top left one. The very soft-spoken images on the far right provide quiet interest on the right side. If this were a painting or fabric art, some adjustments might be considered, such as color or value change on the right side. However, for an impressionistic photo image, making certain the focus is appropriately placed is the most important consideration.

The rule of thirds at work

UNBRIDLED PASSION by Denise Tallon Havlan, Plainfield, Illinois, 49″ × 51″, 2006

Unbridled Passion is an excellent example of the circular focus structure, with the fanciful tree providing the basic rounded shape. This curving shape is reiterated through the careful positioning of the horse's mane, legs, and hooves. The rider's feathered headdress accentuates the top section of the circular structure. The rider with her colorful costume is our stable focal point as our eyes move through the design in a circular clockwise manner.

Circular Structure

Circular structure can be used in two basic ways. First, a central design is the main focus and everything else plays a lesser role, accentuating the beauty of this central design. *Cheddar Cheese, Primrose,* and *Amazon Star* are good examples of this structural focus (pages 21, 37, and 58). When working in this structure, make certain there is enough continuity between the inner focus and the outer support so that the eye can move throughout the design. You don't want the eye trapped in the inner circle, unable to move outward.

The second type of circular structure uses a circular skeleton to move the eyes around the design in a clockwise manner. *Unbridled Passion* is an excellent example of this structure. As you can see, the tree trunk, the horse, its rider, and the detailing of each create a visual circle that our eyes move around. When creating a design such as this, make certain there is interest in each of the design's quadrants. Notice how details in each quadrant were included to create equal distribution of weight, as well as to support the design's imagery.

Triangular Structure

The triangular structure provides a very effective skeleton for designing. You can change the angles of the triangle to accommodate your design quite easily. Two designs that use the triangular structure are *Yellow Daisies* and *Triangles and Beads*. Another example is *Silent Mountain* (page 120). *Autumn Walk* (page 11) uses a triangular structure very innovatively. *It's About Time* (page 61) uses strong value change in an elongated triangular shape to create its design feature and balance.

YELLOW DAISIES by Melinda Bula, El Dorado Hills, California, 18″ × 24″, 2002

Yellow Daisies is an example of the triangular focus structure. In this design our eyes move from one flower to another in a clockwise manner. In this beautifully balanced work of art, Melinda promotes dimensionality by placing her warm-colored yellow flowers against cool green leaves. The warm hues advance while the cool ones recede.

L Structure

The skeleton of the L provides great eye movement, as our eyes follow along the L-shaped structure. In *Cantankerous II* (page 95), you can see how effective the L structure is with regard to flowing eye movement. Our eyes move from the far left redshank to the far right one, and then on to the forward large redshank on the short side of the L. In this structure, as you see in *Cantankerous II*, the major design focus should be along one of the arms of the L. Try to situate the major focus close to the intersecting point of the L rather than at the end of an arm. In *Cantankerous II*, the redshank's head is very close to the intersecting point, providing our eyes with a perfect focus.

Horizontal/Vertical Structure

You can use a horizontal or vertical line as your structure. This directional structure can be used over the entire design surface. *Layers of Time* (page 38) is a beautifully subtle design using a horizontal structure. Also, excellent vertical structure can be seen in *A City Walk in the Spring* (page 84).

TRIANGLES AND BEADS by Ann Fahl, Racine, Wisconsin, 61″ × 47″, 1993

Ann created a very interesting design using the triangular focus structure. It provides a pathway for the movement of our eyes. Notice that the triangular lines are not obvious, but their informal presence allows our eyes to explore the design as they move along the edges of the triangle. To enhance the design, Ann added beads.

SILENT MOUNTAIN by Barbara Anderson Ortiz, Chester, California, 53″ × 56″, 2008

Silent Mountain uses a triangular focus structure to create its design balance. This structure is enhanced by the strong gradation bridge of light and dark values on the mountain, bringing beautiful drama. The gorgeous batiks and hand-dyed fabrics Barbara used provide wonderful visual texture.

ACTIVITIES AND EXERCISES

With every exercise you do in this chapter, select the ratio that works best for the design (pages 77–81). Try to create a design for every ratio, so you can experiment with each. If possible, do each exercise in more than one ratio. It will increase your knowledge of what works within a ratio and it will give you more experience.

1. Look through the artwork in this book. Do you prefer symmetrical or asymmetrical balance? If the former, which type of symmetry do you prefer (pages 108–110)? If you prefer asymmetrical balance, is there a particular structure you prefer (pages 117–120)? Can you determine your preference for balancing visual weight (pages 111–116)? If so, what is your preference?

2. Visit museums, galleries, art shows, and quilt shows. Which designs interest you most? Notice how balance has been attained. What do you like most about your favorites? Do they have a particular structure or way in which focus has been attained? If so, which ones? Write down your findings.

3. Daily, for a month, create little design vignettes using asymmetrical balance (pages 111–120). Play with the following scenarios, finding different ways to create visual weight throughout your design:

a. Balance a large object with other shapes.

b. Balance a brilliantly colored object with other shapes.

c. Balance a lightly colored object with other shapes.

d. Balance a dark object with other shapes.

e. Balance a large, solid-colored object with other shapes.

f. Balance a very textured object with other shapes.

g. Balance a small cluster of objects with other shapes.

4. During a one-week period, create five little design vignettes using the same basic design in each of the following focus structures. The designs will be different because of the focus structure, but there should be basic similarities. Work in any order you wish.

a. Rule of thirds

b. Horizontal structure or vertical structure

c. Triangular structure

d. Circular structure

e. L structure

Repeat using a new basic design for each of the next three weeks.

5. Analyze your past designs. Separate the symmetrical designs from the asymmetrical designs.

a. With the symmetrical designs, which do you like best? Why? What are their strongest features? Did you use any elements and/or principles in such a way as to enhance the design? Would you make any changes if you were to create these designs again? If so, what changes would you make? Write down your findings.

b. Analyze each asymmetrical design from a distance. First, look at each design broadly—not in detail but as a visual overview. Determine what you love about it. What are its strengths? What elements and/or principles did you use that really enhanced the design? What other things do you like about this design? Make a note of your findings.

c. Next, analyze each design with regard to visual weight, balance, and structure. Still view the design from a distance. For each, consider the following questions: Is the weight balanced? If you are not certain, place an imaginary line down the vertical center and assess how much weight is on one side and how much is on the other. If the sides are unequal, how could you weight them better? What changes could you make to redistribute the weight more equitably (for example, change the number of shapes; change the position of shapes; or change the color, texture, or value of shapes)? Now place an imaginary line horizontally across the center. Look at each quadrant. Is there enough interest in each quadrant to attract the eye? If not, how could you bring interest into that quadrant (for example, value or color gradation, additional shapes, and so on)?

Please note: This analysis is not to make you feel bad about past work. It is to give you insight into what you do well and what you want to improve.

6. At least once a month venture outdoors to take photographs of images that will challenge your skills with regard to visual weight in asymmetrical design. It can be challenging to take a well-balanced picture of a flower when it is still attached to its bush and nearby objects are in play. The more you practice extemporaneous shooting with the goal of working with visual balance in asymmetrical design, the more masterful your designs will become in your own medium.

7. Begin planning a new design. Determine the type of balance you will use. Incorporate your favorite elements from earlier chapters. Also, review the design strategies from Chapter 8 (pages 97–107) to determine which unifying principles you might want to include.

Designing Spectacular Quilts

FALL by Mary Louise Parks, Charlotte, North Carolina, 69″ × 81″, 2008

Fall began as an unplanned quilt. Mary was given some Log Cabin blocks by her friend Rhoda Oehser. Not knowing what to do with them, she set them aside. Soon an idea began to simmer in her brain. Mary began by piecing the Log Cabin blocks in a downward diagonal fashion. She finished the quilt in order to use it as a backdrop for a fall woodland scene. She placed the maple and oak trees along the quilt's sides. Then Mary added bushes, logs, flowers, and the forest floor to the quilt's bottom edge, thus creating a visual bridge between the two trees. After the woodland was created, Mary Louise began adding her forest creatures: an owl, a songbird, a fox, two baby foxes hiding behind a log, two pheasants being watched by a cat, two chipmunks, a skunk smelling white flowers, and a partially hidden squirrel reaching for acorns in the oak tree. Imagination is magical! It is amazing to realize that this quilt evolved from a stack of beautifully pieced Log Cabin blocks that were given to a person who had no idea what to do with them … but who was willing to let her imaginative right brain take over the process. I hope this quilt inspires you to let your imagination run wild, as the creative spirit is full of wonderful surprises.

CHAPTER TEN

Important Design Strategies for QUILTS

The process of making a quilt is similar for most of us. When we made our first quilt, we concentrated on the techniques. Then we spent time making quilts for family, friends, our home, and charities. Eventually there comes a day when we yearn to learn more about how to make our quilts more beautiful and how to work more creatively. This chapter provides a broad spectrum of important information related to creating beautiful, well-designed quilts.

A Collection of Basic Design Parameters

DESIGNING FOR YOUR BED

The shape of a bed can play a role in how good a design looks on the bed. When making a bed quilt, select a design that works well for your bed's shape. Because a king-size bed is a square format, large circular designs are beautiful. In addition, intricate block designs and large block designs are great for this bed, as its surface area can handle them.

Designs that work well in a rectangular format are usually beautiful on a queen-size bed. Large circular designs are not appropriate for this shape; instead, this bed's format works better with an elongated circle—an oval. Being a rather narrow rectangle, a twin-size bed looks good with blocks that show good design play in a minimum amount of width. Large circular or oval designs are not good choices for twin-size beds.

Make a paper or computer mockup of your design before beginning any quilt. Be aware of the bed's top design area, since that is where the focus will be. You might draw in the top of the quilt's boundary, so you can see exactly what will be seen on the bed. If you like the way your mockup looks, you are ready to make the quilt. If it needs some adjustments, make the necessary changes. If you don't like the mockup design, begin anew with a different pattern. Making a mockup allows you to become more familiar with the design, to make necessary design changes for your bed's shape, and to make any block adjustments so that the block design works exactly as you want. Mockups eliminate unexpected results and disappointment.

A basic line-drawing mockup may be all you need. However, if it's difficult to see your design in a line drawing, work in a gray value scale. This allows you to concentrate on the actual design. After you have "approved" your overall design, then work with color and/or fabric placement. This can be done rather informally on your worktable or you can add color to your mockup, whichever works better for you. If the latter, you don't have to color the entire drawing; you can just color enough to know what you want to do.

THE HORIZONTAL UNEVEN RULE

With few exceptions, quilt designs look better when the number of blocks in a horizontal row is uneven. Most designs are compromised when an *even* number of blocks is used *horizontally* because the intended focus disappears or appears lost.

Look at the Star Echoes four-block design. Your eyes naturally go to the center. Because there is an even number of blocks horizontally, only block parts can be seen in the center and they hold no real interest or meaning. The featured star is absent from the position of visual honor. Since your eyes naturally focus on the design center, you have to force your eyes to move outward to see a star. Your eyes automatically move back to the center. Unfortunately, this visual dilemma is a major design flaw.

Star Echoes

Star Echoes
four-block design

Star Echoes sixteen-block design

Even with a larger quilt, the eyes still go to the center area. If there is an even number of blocks in a horizontal row, the eyes wander along the vertical center. In this example, we again look at uninteresting block bits because the intended focus, the star, is elsewhere.

Fortunately, this problem can be alleviated easily by using an uneven number of blocks in a horizontal row. When this is done, the viewer's eyes go right to the center and the star is seen. Because the featured element's placement coincides with the eyes' expectations, the eyes feel comfortable. In the nine-block and 25-block designs below, the stars are clearly the focus.

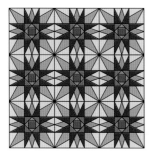

Star Echoes nine-block design

Star Echoes 25-block design

Wedding Wishes is a good example of a quilt following this basic principle, as are *Bali Wedding Star, Memories of Monet, Ticonderoga Star, Big Bang + 1 Second, New Beginnings,* and *California Reel* (pages 36, 54, 78, 94, 130, and 132).

There are a few exceptions to the horizontal uneven rule. If the blocks are small, the rows are numerous, and color or value play are a strong overriding design feature, this principle is not in play, since the eye is captivated by the flow of color or value. In quilts such as *Northern Lights, Postage Stamp Baskets,* and *Plait,* our eyes are focused on the value or color play; the blocks are relatively indiscernible, and the center of the design is a nonissue (pages 20, 29, and 50). *TGIFF (Thank Goodness It's Finally Finished)* (page 125) and *Rainbow* also include a wonderful flow of color.

RAINBOW by Lies Bos-Varkevisser, Enschede, the Netherlands, 60″ × 83″, 2006

Rainbow uses the primary triadic color plan. The entire circle of colors has been incorporated. The multisized stars create unity and variation. With a color-wash quilt such as this, the uneven horizontal rule does not come into play.

WEDDING WISHES by Julie Yaeger Lambert, Erlanger, Kentucky, 51″ × 51″, 2006

Wedding Wishes follows important design principles: It repeats shapes and colors, which results in good visual harmony and unity. It also offers variation and contrast. The design is symmetrical and the motifs are placed in an uneven number horizontally across the design surface, thus allowing us to focus on the center heart design. Julie hand appliquéd and machine pieced this quilt. *Wedding Wishes* is based on a pattern from Jeanna Kimball's book *Red and Green: An Appliqué Tradition.*

TGIFF (THANK GOODNESS IT'S FINALLY FINISHED) by Janyce Broude, Bennington, Vermont, 94″ × 106″, 2007

In *TGIFF*, Janyce challenged herself to work in the Japanese folded-fabric-square technique to create a color-wash quilt using only Asian and solid-color fabrics. With a multitude of small squares placed across this quilt's surface in a colorful wash, there is no requirement to use an even or uneven number of blocks horizontally. Our eyes are attracted to the color movement rather than the individual squares. After completing 750 of the 3¾″ individually hand-quilted squares, Janyce laid 725 of them on the floor and began the process of swapping and replacing. Value play and the primary triadic color plan give this quilt a lively, happy personality.

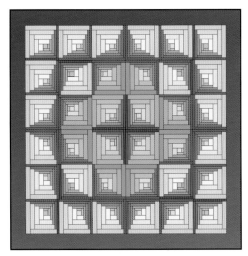

Log Cabin quilts are a notable exception to the horizontal uneven rule, since they need an even number of horizontal blocks for balance. You can see this with the quilts shown on this page.

UNNAMED LOG CABIN by Helen Remick, Seattle, Washington, 90″ × 90″, 1996

Helen uses value masterfully in this glorious Log Cabin quilt. The center area of the quilt uses the contrast of high, middle, and low values to create the main design. The subtle value changes in the outer corners set against the strongly blackened hues create luster and a sense of shimmering. To create this well-balanced design, Helen used an even number of blocks horizontally. The quilt was hand pieced and hand quilted.

Photo by Mark Frey, Yelm, Washington

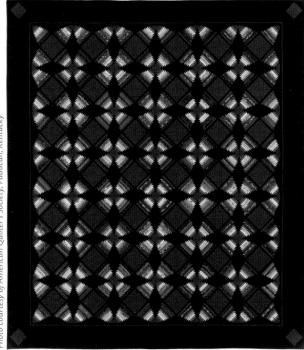

THE ULTIMATE PINEAPPLE by Jane Hall, Raleigh, North Carolina, 76″ × 87″, 1997

Inspired by an antique wool quilt in the Pilgrim/Roy collection of quilts made in the Midwest (circa 1895), Jane created this magnificent Pineapple Log Cabin quilt. The strong value contrast using black, red, and soft ecru gives vibrancy to this quilt.

PERSPECTIVES II by Gloria Hansen, East Windsor, New Jersey, 71″ × 71″, 2001

Perspectives II illustrates the Log Cabin possibilities available to us through imaginative design play. Gloria has created wonderful dimensionality in this Log Cabin quilt, which conveys a very contemporary feeling. Notice that this design needs an even number of blocks horizontally to be balanced.

Photo by the artist

Also, an exception can be made for any block that has interesting shapes in its corners that create a new design when block corners come together. For example, the block Through the Looking Glass has design elements in each corner that result in an interesting design when four corners unite. Therefore, this block can be used in either an even or uneven block setting.

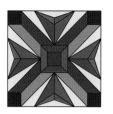

Through the Looking Glass

Through the Looking Glass block copyright © 1994 by Joen Wolfrom

When this block is placed in an even-block setting, our eyes go to the design's center and there is something of interest to see. So, this block works with an even or uneven number of horizontal blocks. There is a slight variation in the design when an even number of horizontal blocks is used compared to an uneven number of blocks. Here the four block corners create a large brown central square that is surrounded by an outer circular design.

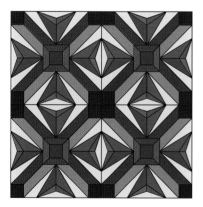

Through the Looking Glass four-block design

When an uneven number of horizontal blocks is used, the block design is featured in the center. In this setting the center is a blue-violet/orange square surrounded by four large petals or star points. This block can be used advantageously with either setting. If you were to select this block for a design, you would determine which center design pleases you most. That decision would dictate whether you use an even or uneven number of horizontal blocks.

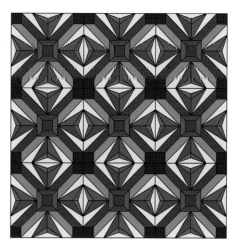

Uneven horizontal block design with nine blocks

FITTING THE BLOCK DESIGN TO THE BED

To reiterate: With few exceptions, plan for an uneven number of blocks horizontally across your bed top (mattress top). This will give your eye a center vertical row to focus on in the middle of the bed. Also, plan to have block edges coincide with the side edges of your bed's top. To do this, determine the width of your mattress (see mattress chart below). Then decide how many blocks will lie horizontally across the *top* of the bed (usually 3, 5, or 7). To determine the block size, divide the mattress width by the number of horizontal blocks on the top of the bed.

EXAMPLES:

Queen bed	King bed
60″ wide	76″ wide
5 blocks across	7 blocks across
60″ ÷ 5 = 12″ block	76″ ÷ 7 = 10.85″ = 11″ block

Type of mattress	Mattress width × length
Crib, six-year	27″ × 52″
Twin, regular	39″ × 75″
Twin, extra long	39″ × 80″
Double (full)	54″ × 75″
Queen	60″ × 80″
King, regular	76″ × 80″
King, dual twin	78″ × 80″

A Block's Skeletal System

Although there are many different types of traditional quilt blocks, most belong to one of the four major block families: four-patch, five-patch, seven-patch, and nine-patch designs. Because the families' skeletal systems are different, each family's designs have some variation and unique characteristics. You may have a preference for one family because of the way its blocks look. Here are the basic differences in their grid systems.

FOUR-PATCH BLOCK DESIGNS

A *four-patch block* begins by dividing a square in half, vertically and horizontally. This creates the basic skeleton of four squares or four patches—hence its name. This basic grid doesn't provide many design options.

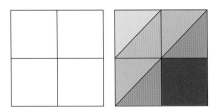

Birds in the Air
Basic four-patch grid: two equal divisions

To expand the options, the square can be divided into four equal divisions, providing 16 grid squares. This simple grid provides for some fun, easy designs, but it may not offer you the design flexibility you want.

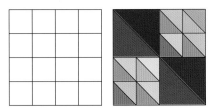

Flock
Simple four-patch grid: four equal divisions

If you divide the square into eight equal divisions, you have the best design flexibility for this family.

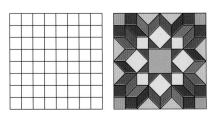

Dutch Rose Variation
Complex four-patch grid: eight equal divisions

FIVE-PATCH BLOCK DESIGNS

A *five-patch block* begins with a square being divided into five equal divisions horizontally and vertically.

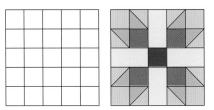

Butterfly at the Crossroad
Simple five-patch grid: five equal divisions

Notice that this block's simple skeleton does not include a center point or centerlines. Instead it has a center grid row that can become a natural lattice in a multiblock design. The basic five-patch grid does not allow great latitude.

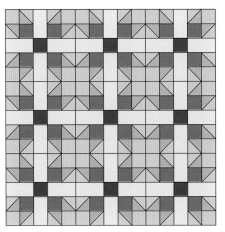

A natural lattice evolves in many five-patch block designs.

If you want more flexibility, make a grid with ten equal divisions.

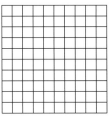 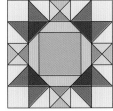

King David's Crown
Complex five-patch grid: ten equal divisions

SEVEN-PATCH BLOCK DESIGNS

A *seven-patch block* begins with a square divided into seven equal divisions. Like the basic five patch grid, there is no center point or line in this basic seven-patch grid. Many of its designs accentuate a lattice made from the center grid rows.

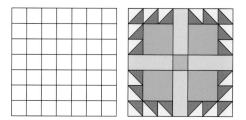

Hen and Chickens
Basic seven-patch grid: seven equal divisions

The complex seven-patch grid of fourteen equal divisions is the most flexible of all the patch-pattern grids. You can create beautiful designs that differ greatly from one another. Both Peacock Dance and Through the Looking Glass (page 127) were created from this grid.

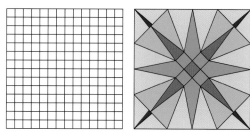

Peacock Dance
Complex seven-patch grid: fourteen equal divisions

Peacock Dance block copyright © 1997 by Joen Wolfrom

NINE-PATCH BLOCK DESIGNS

A *nine-patch block* begins with a square divided into three equal divisions, which makes nine small squares or patches—hence its name. Like the four-patch's basic grid, its basic grid does not leave a lot of opportunities for designing.

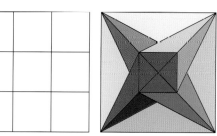

Spinning around the Block
Basic nine-patch: three equal divisions

Spinning around the Block copyright © 1997 by Joen Wolfrom

Six equal divisions provide for many more design options.

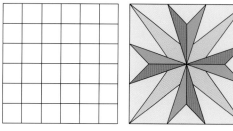

Dancing Star
Simple nine-patch grid: six equal divisions

Dancing Star block copyright © 1996 by Joen Wolfrom

Many beautiful designs can be created from this grid. However, if you need more flexibility, divide the block into twelve equal divisions.

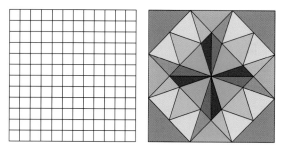

Vermont
Complex nine-patch grid: twelve equal divisions

By selecting a block family and drawing its skeletal lines, you can create hundreds of wonderful patterns for your designs. Making your own designs gives you great latitude. Nowadays you don't have to do it with paper, ruler, and pencil. There are several illustrative software programs that make this task relatively fast and very enjoyable.

Design Strategies

BLENDING BLOCKS

A great way to create intriguing quilts is to use two or more block patterns in one design. If you do this, use block designs from only one grid family. For instance, only work with four-patch designs or only work with nine-patch designs in any one quilt. If you mix block families, you will be disappointed because the shapes will not work well together; the seamlines will not line up. This is because the skeletal grid of each family is different.

Unfortunately, not all blocks in the same family work well together, so you may have to play a bit with different block patterns before you find a design that suits you. Blending two or more blocks together is fun, and you can create some amazing designs. There are several quilts on these pages that blend two or more blocks, including *Memories of Monet, Baskets & Blossoms, Thistle Pods,* and *Ticonderoga Star* (pages 54, 57, 59, and 78). *New Beginnings* and *Nine Patch Stars* (page 131) are also made from blending blocks.

NEW BEGINNINGS by Larisa Key, Willimantic, Connecticut; quilted by Gail B. Federowicz; 68˝ × 86˝, 2006

New Beginnings is a quilt using three slightly varied blocks. These are placed in an on-point setting. With this setting, the design takes on a different, more complex personality. Although each block is created using axes and quadrants, this quilt uses bilateral symmetry to create its design. (Pattern is available.)

Photo by Ken Wagner, Seattle, Washington

BEING BLOCK SAVVY

Selecting blocks that you like and ones that will do what you want in your design is an important first step in beginning your design. Knowing the types of designs you like is also important. Also, recognizing block personalities is an important clue to good block selection.

Some blocks have difficult personalities; they don't like to mix with other blocks. Others are very sociable; they love interacting. Some blocks are shy and need a little help from the designer to be sociable. Because it's difficult to visualize how a block is really going to act or look in a quilt, take time to view your proposed design on paper or on the computer before any rotary cutter touches a piece of fabric. Below are a few hints about block selection.

If a block's motif does not touch its perimeter lines, you should know that this block is an extreme isolationist. It doesn't want to even acknowledge its neighbors.

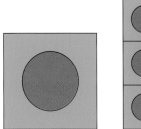 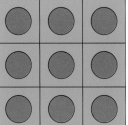

A motif that does not touch the block's perimeter will be isolated in a multiple-block design.

If you love an isolated motif and are up to the challenge, begin figuring out how you can use nature's design elements and principles to bring unity and interest to a quilt made from your selected motif.

Many block patterns do touch their block perimeter lines, but they are either too shy or have no interest in interacting with their neighboring blocks. Star blocks are notorious for being shy. They'll stand at their boundary line but stop short of any type of interaction.

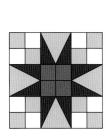 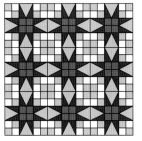

Most star blocks do not interact with their neighbors without some visual prodding.

NINE PATCH STARS by Judy Spiers, Foxworth, Mississippi, 19" × 19", 2006

Nine Patch Stars, a multiple-award-winning miniature quilt, is filled with tiny shapes and superb intricacy. It has both unity and contrast. The red, yellow, and black shapes run throughout the design, creating good repetition and rhythm and resulting in unity while the blue motif creates contrasting interest. Our eyes are attracted to the central design in this well-balanced, blended-block quilt.

It is possible to encourage these shy beauties to become sociable. Color and value are two enticing design elements that promote interaction. Also, adding design lines can be a very ingenious way to entice an isolated block to interact. Study the different ways designers have tackled this design challenge.

Quilts using color and/or value to create interaction include *Moonsnail, The Colour of Jazz,* and *Big Bang + 1 Second* (pages 36, 61, and 94). *Tropical Radiance* (page 10), a four-pointed star block design, has added echo lines. *Jewel's Garden* (page 133) uses a subtle lattice to move from one four-pointed star to another. In *California Reel,* each block seems to be hugging its neighbor, as the motifs wrap around each other. *Bali Wedding Star* (page 36) is a stunning example of each star reaching out to embrace its neighbor through additional design lines. These quilt designers have masterfully concealed their blocks' isolating tendencies, and in doing so have created amazing designs.

If you would prefer not to challenge yourself with blocks that need special attention and prodding, select blocks that have *open arms.* Open arms are openings along a block's perimeter where two blocks can visually connect. This allows for interesting design possibilities.

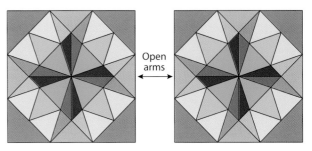

Look for designs with open arms—places where two blocks will visually connect to create interesting interaction.

When open-armed blocks are united, intriguing designs evolve. There is great probability that these designs will have excellent interaction.

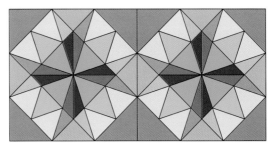

The two blocks unite with their open arms. When this happens, interesting designs evolve.

CALIFORNIA REEL by Allison Alexis Lockwood, Shell Beach, California, 86″ × 86″, 2001

California Reel is an original design by Allison, inspired by the Virginia Reel block. One of the beautiful characteristics of this design is the block's interactive quality. Its beauty is enhanced by the fact that Allison used an uneven number of horizontal blocks, thus allowing the full potential of this design to come forth.

JEWEL'S GARDEN by Judy Mercer Tescher, Pendleton, Indiana, 60″ × 80″, 1999

Filled with harmonic unity and contrast, this beautiful quilt is a tribute to Judy's mother, Jewel, and her love of flowers and gardening. The wonderful interaction between blocks in *Jewel's Garden* is promoted by the use of the subtle latticework that seemingly moves from one four-pointed star to another.

Photo by Ellen Tescher Nolan

Another clue for good block interaction is a block's corner shapes. If a block has interesting shapes moving into its corners, then new designs may evolve when blocks unite. One day I drew fat corner shapes in a block, not knowing what would happen. The block turned out too clunky for my taste, so I was rather disappointed with it.

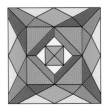

Poinsettia in Bloom
This block seemed too clunky to amount to much designwise.

Poinsettia in Bloom block by Joen Wolfrom, Fox Island, Washington, 1997

Before discarding the block, I decided to see how it interacted with neighboring blocks. You can imagine my surprise when I put the blocks together and found stars, circles, and unexpected movement. Hence, Poinsettia in Bloom was born.

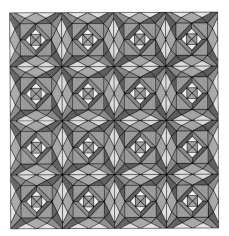

Surprising stars and circles evolved when the blocks were put together.

This type of design surprise is one of the reasons I believe wholeheartedly in design play. It's difficult to know how a design will work when you have only one block before you. I like to work with 25 blocks (a 5 block × 5 block mockup). This allows me to see a design's possibilities and any needed adjustments.

If you love illusionary curves and movement in your designs, consider inviting equilateral, acute, scalene, or obtuse triangles into your designs. Although half-square and quarter-square triangles are the most popular triangles for quilters, they do not promote the illusion of curves or movement.

DIAGONAL BLOCK SETTINGS— GOING ON-POINT

Placing blocks in a diagonal setting often enhances a design. *Star of Wonder* (page 8) is made from a pattern called Star Echoes (page 123). Linda Crouch-McCreadie decided to change the design by placing the blocks on point. This simple change gave the star a gracefully elegant makeover. Another example of an on-point (diagonal) setting is *Feathered Baskets*. Other examples are *Bear Tracks in the Garden* and *LeMoyne Star & Friends* (both on page 135).

If you want a diagonal setting for your block pattern, make this decision *prior* to making your quilt blocks. Placing a block in a diagonal position increases its horizontal width by 1.414 (the square root of 2). A 10″ block becomes a 14.14″ block when set on the diagonal (10″ × 1.414 = 14.14″). If you don't plan ahead by resizing the block, your quilt will become larger than your bed may be able to accommodate. Eight block sizes and their approximate diagonal conversions are on page 135.

FEATHERED BASKETS by Larisa Key, Willimantic, Connecticut; quilted by Wilma Cogliantry; 80″ × 98″, 2006

In *Feathered Baskets*, Larisa surrounds the central medallion flower design with on-point basket blocks. By placing the light-value blocks along the quilt's outer edge, she creates a strong value contrast between the overall design and the border. The central design is both clearly defined and visually balanced. Consequently, the visual interest remains within the central design.

BLOCK SIZE AND DIAGONAL BLOCK MEASUREMENT CONVERSION

Block size	Diagonal block
6″	8½″
8″	11⁵⁄₁₆″
10″	14⅛″
11″	15⁹⁄₁₆″
12″	17″
18″	25½″
20″	28¼″
24″	33¹⁵⁄₁₆″

BEAR TRACKS IN THE GARDEN by Larisa Key, Willimatic, Connecticut; quilted by Gail B. Federowicz; 77″ × 105″, 2005

This stunning one-block design by Larisa has been placed on the diagonal, which enhances its beauty. (Rotate the quilt to see what the design would look like if it were not placed on the diagonal.) Notice the airiness of this design, which is created because the pointed shapes do not meet from one block to the next. (Pattern is available.)

Photo by Ken Wagner, Seattle, Washington

LEMOYNE STAR & FRIENDS by Sharyn Craig, El Cahon, California, 72″ × 72″, 1998

Creating a sampler quilt is a challenge because there is so much variation in shape, visual weight, color, style, and fabric between the blocks. Sharyn has brought unity to this sampler quilt through repetition of color, fabrics, and value. Additionally, she has controlled the imagery by limiting the blocks to star designs. Adding the diagonal lattice holds the stars together in a frame, while the simple border repeating the value range allows our eyes to stay comfortably in the design.

ADDING DIMENSIONALITY IN YOUR QUILTS

One of the most significant enhancements you can make to your quilt designs is to add dimensionality. To begin, analyze your block pattern to see how many layers it has—or how many layers you want to use. For an example, look at the Mexican Cross block.

Mexican Cross with three layers

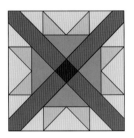

Mexican Cross with four layers

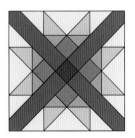

Mexican Cross with five layers

In the first Mexican Cross block example, three design layers are used: the diagonal lattice, the complete star, and the background. In the second example, there are four layers. The additional layer creates more interest. The lighter and grayer properties create a sense of dimensionality. In the third example, there are five design layers. This is the most interesting block, as the illusion of depth is more captivating with these multiple layers. The first block example looks flat in comparison. Which block layering would you prefer for a design strategy?

In *Memories of Monet* (page 54), there are three layers: the foreground four-pointed stars, the softly colored diagonal lattice, and the background. The diagonal lattice looks like it is behind the stars because the fabrics used are lighter, grayer, and less distinct than those used for the stars. The background fabrics are mostly lighter, grayer, and less distinct than the lattice fabrics, and therefore recede farther into the distance.

In summary, if you want to incorporate depth in your quilts, the first (top) layer should be the strongest in coloring and the most distinct in detail and texture. The next layer should be lighter in value, grayer in coloring, and less distinct in detail and texture than the first layer. Each receding layer should be lighter, grayer, and less distinct than the one preceding it. If you want a layer to appear close to another layer, make these changes subtle. If you want clear differences in your layers, make the changes pronounced. You can have both subtle and pronounced layers within one design.

USING A BLOCK PATTERN TO CREATE UNRELATED DESIGNS

It is fun to use a block pattern's shapes to create a totally unrelated design. *Snail Mail* is a charmingly whimsical quilt utilizing this idea. The sky and foreground are pieced using the traditional block Snail Trail. The snail, mailbox, and letter are appliquéd.

SNAIL MAIL by Gwyned Trefethen, Appleton, Wisconsin, 24″ × 24″, 2006

Snail Mail is a delightful quilt that uses the traditional pattern Snail Trail to create the sky and foreground. Gwyned's snail, mailbox, and letter were appliquéd. This quilt toured with the themed exhibit Doing Small Things with Great Love in 2006.

Similarly, *Majestic Mountains* is a design created from the Storm at Sea block. The shapes of the mountains, foothills, luminous sunset, and water are based on the shapes provided in the Storm at Sea block.

MAJESTIC MOUNTAINS by Joen Wolfrom,
Fox Island, Washington, 60″ × 48″, 2005

This mountain scene was created by using the four-patch Storm at Sea block. The block shapes are the vehicle to create this design.

Another example of using blocks and their shapes to create innovative quilts is *Good Old Mountain Music Memories*. Linda Kaiser used two blocks to create a backdrop for her celebration of country music.

GOOD OLD MOUNTAIN MUSIC MEMORIES by Linda Kaiser, Jonesborough, Tennessee, 42″ × 42″, 2008

Using the two blocks Tennessee Waltz and Down Home Rag, Linda created an innovative quilt that celebrates the joys of mountain music. Using traditional blocks in nontraditional ways is both fun and creatively freeing. You can almost hear the music coming from this happy quilt.

Border Basics

The purpose of a border is to provide visual closure for your quilt. In essence, a border should stop the eye from moving outward and bring the eye back to the body of the quilt—the main design. Its role is similar to that of a picture frame. It should not overpower the design it surrounds. For this task to be performed well, an obvious element from the design must be repeated in the border in order to bring about unity between the two parts. Borders become complicated when more than one element is invited to be part of the framing. To make certain that borders attend to their task and do not overwhelm the design, there are guidelines to follow that are based on design principles.

MANAGING YOUR BORDER

First, it is not essential to have a border on your quilt. Scenic quilts rarely need borders. Many designs in this book have no borders.

A plain border using the quilt's main color usually works beautifully. It stops the eye and takes it back to the quilt's center. It does its job effectively and simply—much like a picture frame. A multicolored border can add an accent, if needed, similar to the matting used in framing. The dominant color in the quilt should be given the dominant border role. Each color should have the same prominence in the border as it does in the quilt. One color should not upstage another because of its placement in the border.

The border should only include colors, values, and shapes from the design. Any new idea or change in shape, color, or value will attract the eye immediately. If you use shapes in your border, they should not be larger than the shapes in your design. If they are, your eyes will become more attracted to them than to the ones in your design.

When a border is out of proportion or has attracted attention with new elements, it is in competition with the design. If it becomes the dominant attraction, visual conflict arises. The border should never take over the design's role. This would be a major design flaw.

SIZING YOUR BORDER

To keep the border under control, plan to have its width no more than half the size of the block. Thus, if your block is 12″ wide, use a maximum border width that is approximately 6″. A little fudging upward is visually acceptable, but if you make the border closer to the block width, it will begin to compete with the design in the body of the quilt.

If you are making a medallion quilt, the central design should be strong enough to accommodate the surrounding borders. Each border side should be less than the central design's width. Try to keep the combination of side borders closer to half the width of the central design, if possible. If that is not possible, as you work keep stepping back to view your design from a distance to make certain you are not giving the borders more importance than the central medallion has. If the border is too wide and attention-grabbing for the medallion center, it will take over the dominant role. Again, the medallion center should be the dominant focus, not the borders.

Bright Hopes, an elegant medallion quilt, is an excellent example of border planning. All the border shapes and units reiterate one or more elements from the central design. The colors, values, and fabrics in the border are ones used in the medallion center. As a result, *Bright Hopes* shows beautiful unity. The border enhances the central design.

BRIGHT HOPES by Karen Kay Buckley, Carlisle, Pennsylvania, 88″ × 88″, 2003

In this elegant medallion quilt, all the border shapes and motifs reiterate one or more elements from the central medallion design. Each border plays with these in its own way. By using the central design for the border elements, beautiful unity is created and the medallion remains the central focus.

Photo by Joseph Buckley, Carlisle, Pennsylvania

BORDER INNOVATIONS

If you design an innovative border, make certain there is continuity between it and the body of your quilt. Be sure to incorporate the design guidelines with your creative treatment, since it can be very easy to let an innovative border dominate the design.

Having some parts of your design flow into the border brings added interest, extends your design surface, and can be visually intriguing. *Moonlight Sonata, Dresden Flower Garden,* and *Friends in High Places* are enhanced by this border treatment (pages 49, 89, and 111), as is *Birdland. Tropical Radiance* (page 10) effectively uses a mock border to bring closure to its design. Look through the book to see the different border treatments used. Observe what borders work best and how they were designed.

BIRDLAND by Laura Wasilowski, Elgin, Illinois, 40″ × 51″, 2002

This wonderfully fanciful quilt uses an uneven number of birdhouses, which helps to create good natural balance. *Birdland* also illustrates how a design can be extended into a border, thereby increasing the informal width of the design.

Photo by George Tarbay, DeKalb, Illinois

In the Spirit of Quilting

There are many spectacular quilts included within these pages that combine originality with design elements and principles. They vary greatly in style and creative flair. Look through the book to see what most appeals to you. Take note of the elements and design principles that you particularly like in these quilts. That will help give you a point from which to begin designing your future quilts.

For many decades, the technical aspects of quiltmaking have overshadowed the importance of design. However, the two are really a partnership. It's unfortunate if a quilt is technically perfect but visually uninteresting. Conversely, it's a problem if the design is stunning but the workmanship is too carefree. So, making a beautiful, successful quilt requires both technical and design skills. I hope you will be inspired to experiment with the elements and principles of design as they relate to your creative dreams. The more you learn about design, the more fun designing becomes.

When working on your own projects, be open to ideas that pop into your head, no matter how wild and wacky they may seem. This is your creative brain giving you important clues and messages. Each step in your designing leads you farther down the path to where you want to be. When you make mistakes, greet them in good spirit, as mistakes lead to innovation, experimental learning, and growth. Remember: perfection and creativity do not go hand in hand. If you demand perfection of yourself, it makes it very difficult for your creativity to flow. Be generous and positive about the progress you make. Give it your best effort. Who can ask for more?

When designing your quilts, have fun, have faith in your own talents, and enjoy the adventure. Happy designing!

Joen

ACTIVITIES AND EXERCISES

1. After reading the chapters on elements and principles, look at the quilts you have made. Divide them into two groups: the ones you love and the ones you wish had turned out differently. Look at the first group and write down all the things you feel you did well. Note why you think these quilts work well visually. With the second group, write down the reasons you think they did not work. Consider all the different design concepts covered in earlier chapters as well as this chapter.

2. With your personal critique in mind, decide what types of quilts you would like to make in the near future. Jot down all the ideas you would like to try. After you have brainstormed, select the ideas that seem most doable for your next quilt. Plan your quilt; explore ways to implement your plan. On paper or using a computer program, make a mockup of your quilt design. Do not be overly concerned about getting the colors exactly right on your mockup. You just want an impression of how the colors and values will work.

3. If you want to begin designing your own blocks, select a quilt block that gives you some basic lines that you like. (If you have a quilt-design computer program, use it for this exercise.) Enlarge the block to at least 8″ square. Include the block's grid lines. Then draw the block's design lines. Make several copies.

Add lines to the design. Eliminate lines you don't want. As you add and remove lines, a new design will evolve. Once you complete one block, create a completely different variation with another copy. Select your best designs. Resize blocks to 2″ square. Make enough copies to have 9 (3 blocks × 3 blocks) or 25 blocks (5 blocks × 5 blocks). You get a glimpse of the design possibilities with 9 blocks; making 25 blocks allows you to see the design much more clearly. Cut and paste the blocks to create paper quilts. Put the paper quilts on the wall. Stand back and analyze the designs. Do you need to add more lines? If so, add them. Are there distracting lines? If so, eliminate them. Then redo, print, cut, paste, and analyze again.

NOTE

For a quick look at your design after it's scaled down, place two mirrors at right angles together next to one block. Look in the mirrors and you will see a multiple-block design. You can see immediately whether the design is good or whether you need to make some adjustments.

4. If you are a quilter who wants to create a design using geometric shapes as your vehicle, select a quilt block that gives you flexibility but not too much complexity. Scale the block to 1″ square. Print 25 copies of the block; then cut and paste the blocks into 5 rows of 5 blocks (or copy, cut, and paste a different number of blocks). Print several copies of this paper quilt. With colored pencils, watercolor pencils, or paint, create an overall design. Avoid thinking or working block by block. Instead, focus on the total surface. When you construct this design, you can work in rows, units, or blocks, using your "design map" as your visual guide. Allow changes as you go.

5. If you have access to a quilt-design computer program, select a grid block family to use for designing blended-block quilts. Select one block that you really like in that family. Then select several other blocks that might make good partners. Make an imaginary quilt using your favorite block along with each of the other selected blocks. If you like one or more combinations, play with different design ideas using these blocks. Save them in a file to begin a blended-block design collection. As time permits, select a blended-block design to begin a quilt.

SUBJECT INDEX

INDEX OF CONTRIBUTORS

About the Author

After leaving her career in the educational field to become a homemaker in 1974, Joen became interested in quilt-making and textile art. During a span of fifteen years, she created commissioned textile art for private clients and corporations. Her work is included in collections throughout the world.

As a guest lecturer/instructor on the subject of color and design, Joen has taught throughout the United States and in England, the Republic of Ireland, Northern Ireland, Scotland, Canada, Germany, the Netherlands, Taiwan, Australia, New Zealand, and South Africa.

Joen is the author of twelve previously published books and products. Several have been best sellers in the art/craft field; some have been translated into other languages. Her published works include *Color Play, The Visual Dance, The Magical Effects of Color, Visual Coloring,* and *Landscapes & Illusions,* as well as invaluable products such as Ultimate 3-in-1 Color Tool, Studio Color Wheel, and Design-Ratio Tool.

Joen is the owner of JWD Publishing, a pattern company that publishes quilt-related patterns. She enjoys photography, reading, traveling, and spending time with her family.

Correspondence may be sent directly to Joen at 104 Bon Bluff, Fox Island, Washington 98333. You may visit Joen's website at www.joenwolfrom.com or her pattern company's website at www.jwdpublishing.com.

BIBLIOGRAPHY

Doczi, György. *The Power of Limits: Proportional Harmonies in Nature, Art and Architecture.* Boston, Massachusetts: Shambhala, 1981.

Dow, Arthur Wesley. *Composition, Understanding Line, Notan and Color.* Mineola, New York: Dover Publications, 2007, unabridged republication of the 9th edition.

Elam, Kimberly. *Geometry of Design.* New York, New York: Princeton Architectural Press, 2001.

Poore, Henry Rankin. *Pictorial Composition: An Introduction.* Mineola, New York: Dover Publications, 1976.

Roberts, Ian. *Mastering Composition.* Cincinnati, Ohio: North Light Books, 2007.

Schulzke, Margot. *A Painter's Guide to Design and Composition.* Cincinnati, Ohio: North Light Books, 2006.

Wolfrom, Joen. *The Visual Dance.* Concord, California: C&T Publishing, 1995.

Other books and products by Joen Wolfrom

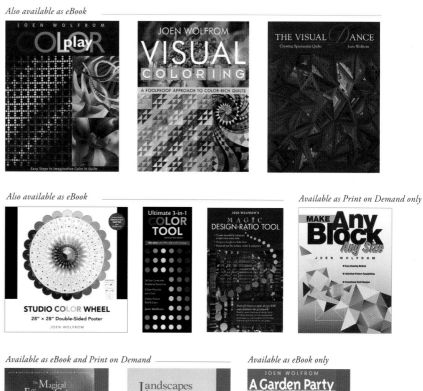

Great Titles *from* C&T PUBLISHING and stashBOOKS®

Available at your local retailer or **www.ctpub.com** *or* **800-284-1114**